Implementing
Global
Networked
Systems
Management:
Strategies and Solutions

The McGraw-Hill Series on Computer Communications
(Selected Titles)

Implementing Global Networked Systems Management:
Strategies and Solutions

Raj Ananthanpillai

McGraw-Hill
New York • San Francisco • Washington, D.C. • Auckland
Bogotá • Caracas • Lisbon • London • Madrid • Mexico City
Milan • Montreal • New Delhi • San Juan • Singapore
Sydney • Tokyo • Toronto

Library of Congress Cataloging-in-Publication Data

Ananthanpillai, Raj.
    Implementing global networked systems management : strategies and
solutions / Raj Ananthanpillai..
        p.   cm.
    Includes index.
    ISBN 0-07-001601-1
        1. Wide area networks—Management. 2. Business—Communication
systems—Data processing. 3. Communication, International.
I. Title.
TK5105.87.A53   1997
004'.36—dc21   97-22889
                                                               CIP

McGraw-Hill

A Division of The McGraw-Hill Companies

1 2 3 4 5 6 7 8 9 0   DOC/DOC   9 0 2 1 0 9 8 7

ISBN 0-07-001601-1

The sponsoring editor for this book was *Steve Elliot* and the production supervisor was *Tina Cameron*. It was designed, edited, and set in Vendome ICG and Eras by *TopDesk Publishers' Group*.

Printed and bound by *R. R. Donnelley & Sons Company*.

This book is printed on recycled, acid-free paper containing a minimum of 50% recycled, de-inked fiber.

McGraw-Hill books are available at special quantity discounts to use as premiums and sales promotions, or for use in corporate training programs. For more information, please write to the Director of Special Sales, McGraw-Hill, 11 West 19th Street, New York, NY 10011. Or contact your local bookstore.

To my family
Radhika, Rekha, Raman,
and my Parents

CONTENTS

Contents

PREFACE

Global corporations are undergoing a fundamental change in how they do business. There is a tidal wave movement from older mainframe-centric information infrastructures towards client/server and distributed architectures. Information networks are being extended and expanded globally to accommodate the efforts of organizations to globalize their business. Networking systems globalization and the spread of distributed, client/server technology introduce new variables never before conceived of nor planned for. The most important challenge is managing such globally distributed information networks and the associated distributed and mission-critical applications. More often than not, these networks are upgraded by carrying along with them their previous network and systems management tools and processes.

As users migrate their computer resources from centralized to distributed client/server environments, managing these resources has become exponentially more costly and complex. Adding to the complexity are the increasing number and types of different system resources, configuration changes, and the delegation of more management functionality to the desktop. How do you manage multiple server sites efficiently and effectively? How do you manage multiple databases and operating systems? How do you keep distributed systems management costs from overriding the gains in productivity that prompted the move to a distributed environment in the first place? One strategy is to select an integrated network and systems management framework upon which to build an effective enterprise-wide, networked system management solution.

When information technology (IT) departments were organized along technology lines, systems management responsibilities were divided among systems managers, network managers, data administrators, and applications specialists. As the move to distributed systems extends across the enterprise, these management disciplines are converging. For example, performance management was once handled by systems performance experts who tuned and optimized the system by maximizing host CPU performance. In today's distributed environment, if a user is experiencing poor performance with a client/server application that incorporates multiple servers across disparate network links, diagnosing that problem will require analysis and assessment of multiple components (servers, client, network links, applications status, and database management systems [DBMS])—not just the host CPU. Hence, distributed computing requires a cross-disciplinary management approach, whereby administrators must correlate the separate systems, network, database, and applications administrative facilities to manage the problem.

Networking management products are used to monitor the physical network, logical network, and networking devices and components. Systems management products are used to control, monitor, and manage operating systems, network services, and applications services. Database administration applications are used to optimize performance and manage database operational activities. The lack of integration between these products has resulted not only in replication of effort, but also in costly and inefficient problem resolution and enterprise operations management.

Meanwhile, organizations new to client/server computing expect a complete set of management tools, similar to those found in mainframe environments. However, these organizations soon learn that the traditional, glass-house mainframe-centric systems management methods and tools are not normally transferable to distributed environments. As they attempt to mix and match available off-the-shelf systems management software (point solutions) as well as home-grown solutions, administrative costs are surpassing the costs of distributed system implementation. These costs include additional administrative personnel; integration, training, and other hidden costs of off-the-shelf systems management software; and custom development of systems management tools, which diverts programming resources from end-user applications. See Figure I (below) for operations cost anomalies as IT complexities increase.

Figure I

Operational Costs Anomolies in a Distributed Systems Environment

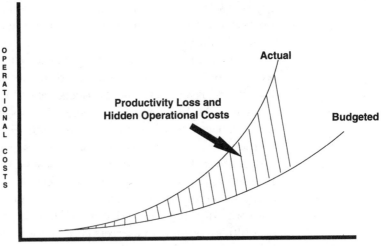

Actual

Productivity Loss and Hidden Operational Costs

Budgeted

OPERATIONAL COSTS

INFORMATION TECHNOLOGY COMPLEXITY

Most distributed systems management products do not support the client/server heterogeneous environment but are platform specific (a platform is a set of infrastructure components for network and systems management applications and operations). Platform dependence forces users to take a three-pronged approach; i.e., they must switch between system, DBMS, and network management products. What is required is an enterprise-wide system management solution that is consistent across multiple disparate platforms, provides a common methodology and interface, displays standardized performance metrics, and provides comprehensive graphical reporting techniques to communicate with management and users. The solution must also be capable of automating management tasks wherever possible, or delegating them to the appropriate off-site servers.

A distributed systems management framework is a set of technologies and processes that enables organizations to manage distributed networks of computers from multiple vendors. It provides a foundation for management tools for heterogeneous computing environments. A distributed system management framework enables the development of management service applications independent of the underlying hardware or operating systems. Framework middleware provides the means for systems management applications to interoperate across the enterprise with a high degree of independence from the underlying network protocol and hardware platforms. Included are application programming interface (API) services that facilitate third-party and end-user development of management applications by providing a consistent interface to different hardware platforms, operating systems, system resources, and management tasks. They also provide a consistent way of applying management policies to create custom applications. Thus, the distributed systems management framework provides the middleware for distributed systems management applications products, isolating these products from platform-specific interfaces, facilitating movement across multiple platforms, implementing multiple systems management disciplines, and providing portability across environments and emerging standards.

Two types of applications products are required to manage distributed environments: distributed operations management and distributed systems administration. Distributed operations management applications focus on maintaining and increasing the productivity of computing resources across distributed environments, through such tasks as system performance monitoring, workload scheduling, storage management, security management, and problem resolution. Distributed systems administration applications focus on increasing the productivity of systems administrators by allowing them to better deal with end-user requirements. Administration applications involve user/group management, managing distributed services such as electronic mail and printing services, operating system configuration, software distribution, and database administration.

Distributed operations management should focus on improving availability while containing support costs. It provides access to, and control over, the entire distributed systems environment, integrating systems, databases, and network management from a centralized management console. The management console should address the entire distributed systems environment and monitor domains that span the entire enterprise, such as servers and clients for a particular application, region, department, or administrator. Central management of multiple servers in a network provides a single, consistent environment for performing all systems administration tasks, masking the differences among hardware and operating platforms. From the console, users can filter, schedule actions, and store messages that originated from the operating systems or from applications. Automated console interaction allows the system to identify console messages, both input and output, that are to be selected for processing by the systems management program, and schedule activities based upon time of day and event conditions.

A common mistake that designers of networks commit is to leave the problem of identifying the networking management tools and system to the network operations organization. It is extremely important for someone other than in network operations to take a look at what is needed for managing the network from end to end, not only today but for years to come. More often than not, network operations are focused on their current problems (usually due to their job descriptions!) and seek out solutions for their short-term productivity improvements. It is very important to establish an architecture and a framework for integrated networking management before jumping to identifying technology and systems solutions.

Investments in new network management systems and technology should be justified by increased management staff productivity, increased network reliability, availability, and serviceability, and, above all, better control over a mission-critical infrastructure of the business. A common mistake is to justify new network management systems and technology to reduce operations staff. This reduction rarely happens and, instead, the operators tend to spend more time learning and dealing with the new technology. However, in the long run the network operations staffing needs do not grow proportionally to the expansion and growth of the underlying networks themselves. Intelligent and integrated networking management is a continuum, and users and designers should carefully examine different claims of "integration." A basic level is sharing menus and the GUI, giving all tools the same look and feel. While this improves the network operator's functions a lot, it falls far short of "effectively" managing the network, which requires data-level integration driven by a common management information repository and an inference engine.

This book does not describe a panacea. I wrote it to meet a real need for managing globally distributed complex networks. And it is that pragmatic approach to achieving results and managing real-world complex networks from end to end that is sometimes missing from the current formal standards bodies and vendors providing disparate products and services. It is extremely important for the end-user to move away from "vertical thinking" and focus and expand on "systems thinking"—a move that will address not only vertical network management needs but also horizontal integrated network management needs. It is this vision that led me to write this book.

As client/server computing extends throughout the enterprise, users need comprehensive tools to manage the entire distributed environment. Distributed computing requires a single interface and tool set that can manage heterogeneous databases, networks, applications, and operating systems; automate routine systems administration tasks for distributed systems management; and comply with evolving standards. The distributed systems management framework described in this book provides users with these requirements. Hence, in planning for distributed systems management, one should choose operations management products that can be integrated within a distributed systems management framework, choose a database whose administration tools can also plug into the framework, and design applications so that the standardized agents and protocols are used to report events rather than relying on application-specific log files.

Throughout this book several terms are used interchangeably. Networking management, network and systems management, networked systems management, distributed systems management, and management of distributed networks all refer to the same problems and issues related to networks and systems that are distributed both locally and/or globally, and are interconnected using communications and computing technologies.

In writing this book, I have chosen to speak to varied audiences, including strategists and senior managers concerned about the escalating costs of managing and operating their distributed environment, and practicing managers responsible for designing, managing, and operating their distributed networks. A sizable portion of the book provides strategies for management to evaluate and incorporate in their efforts to globally expand their IT infrastructure.

I believe this book offers an approach to the design, development, and implementation of network and systems management infrastructure that demystifies the process of theory building and shows how it is possible for practitioners to become their own theorists, developing penetrating strategies and solutions about how to manage their ever-changing, complex distributed networked systems.

—RAJ ANANTHANPILLAI

ACKNOWLEDGMENTS

No book consists solely of the efforts of its author. This book is certainly no exception, especially since it grew out of my collective experiences at AT&T and I-NET. I continue to draw inspiration from Dale DeJager, my coach from my AT&T days. As a compendium of systemic management wisdom, *Implementing Global Networked Systems Management: Strategies and Solutions* owes an enormous debt to the many professionals and senior executives in corporate America whose constant quest for better manageability of their information systems infrastructure has advanced the state of networked systems management.

The following individuals deserve special mention. Ken Bajaj at I-NET provided me the opportunity to develop and practice certain concepts detailed in this book. Some of the systems, such as common management information repository (CMIR), were developed during my days at I-NET and proved to be a tremendous success with the customers and users. Rita Roche and Amanda Toone helped me immensely over the past year or so in developing the figures contained in this book. I also want to mention that Steve Elliot, my editor at McGraw-Hill, has been a constant source of irritation over the past few months. Thank you, Steve. Without your gentle prodding, I am sure that I would have never finished this tome.

Finally, I want to thank my family from the bottom of my heart for the sacrifice they made on behalf of this book. Radhika, my wife, deserves special thanks for putting up with my frequent absence from home during and after our latest addition to the family, our son, Raman. Rekha, our seven-year-old daughter, who innocently kept asking when I would finish this book and play with her more, was, in her own way, helpful in speeding up the development of this book. My parents and my brothers always deserve special thanks for their continuous encouragement and support.

Implementing
Global
Networked
Systems
Management:
Strategies and Solutions

CHAPTER 1

Introduction

Global corporations, both in service and in manufacturing industries, are applying technology to network their information movement and business transactions to gain a competitive edge in the marketplace. Some vertical industries in financial services, airlines, and manufacturing are leading this wave as their business practices have established protocols and formalized transactions. With the rapid improvements in computers and communications, however, more and more activities of other industries are utilizing network technology to move their information globally to take advantage of services with the lowest total cost. Concurrently, the landscape of information technology development is changing at a faster pace. Existing and nearly completed public national data networks and public or quasi-public regional and international networks in virtually all developed and several developing countries have spurred rapid growth in data-service industries.

Today, global corporations rely on data-service industries and information technology not only to speed up business transactions, but also to improve corporate management and control by improving corporate functions such as financial control, strategic planning, inventory control, and changing the manner of production. Global corporations' processes for planning, control and coordination, and reporting depend increasingly on information technology. In essence, the corporations' lifeline depends on moving and managing the information necessary to drive the business. Thus, the systems and applications that ride on the network become the linchpin for the corporations: in effect, the network becomes the system.

Information networking is a strong force that will continue to force countries around the world towards a global market economy, restructuring corporations, and bringing countries around the world closer together. This whirlwind will integrate computers, telephony, and people (processes) into a common network, a central nervous system for a global society. For their information systems, global corporations are moving from the previous monolithic mainframe operations towards distributed client/server systems. Information networks are moving from being domestic and international to being global and multiregional. These movements introduce new variables never before conceived of nor planned for. One of the most important challenges is managing such globally distributed information systems and networks. More often than not these networks and systems, while upgraded and enhanced using new technology, carry along earlier versions of their management architecture, tools, and systems. These architectures, systems, and paradigms are not only outdated but also decrease the productivity of information systems, thus leading to frustrations with new technology and perhaps ultimately to the failure of the business itself. Predicting problems and issues in a globally distributed network is a luxury, given today's dynamic and complex business world. Sole reliance on experience and on existing tools and systems may cause one to overlook critical new challenges and fail to provide the necessary information management systems and decision support systems. These pitfalls can be avoided by establishing a vision that is in alignment with the underlying information systems architecture, a cohesive approach, and a new paradigm for managing such systems and networks.

Corporate success in this and the coming decades will increasingly depend on the ability to effectively exploit distributed information resources and computing power for competitive advantage. With communication systems thus becoming the lifeline of today's corporations, ways to manage and control those systems and the underlying networks have become of paramount concern. Thus, these new-generation information systems necessitate a shift in the traditional approaches to network and systems management, including the responsibilities of managers of enterprise networks. In addition, technology refreshment and "value" creation should be additional drivers to develop an enterprise management framework for managing the information infrastructure and systems. Development of an enterprise management system is especially challenging while the re-engineering of the underlying infrastructure and the systems and applications that ride on them are undertaken to make it useful to the corporation that is now a global player. The management systems for the globally distributed information networks need to support both flexibility in and coordination among a company's diverse activities in the new international markets.

It is very important first of all to understand the business and organization of the corporation and its current information systems architecture. Without a thorough understanding of this, it is difficult to develop a whole system architecture for managing the enterprises' information systems end-to-end.

Overview of Information Revolution

Whereas during the Industrial Revolution corporations had to excel in production and manufacturing techniques, in the Information Revolution they have to obtain flawless coordination among business functions. This is because businesses are beginning to change dramatically due to significant advances in miniaturization and transmission technologies. Computers and communication networks allow us to move, store, and process information faster, more cheaply, and over greater distances than ever before. This phenomenon, known in the industry as *MIPS and BAUD costs becoming insignificant,* has already led to the creation of new industries, to the accumulation of new wealth, and to changes in almost all kinds of business. Businesses must arrange to have the right things in the right places at the right times. They must decide what to do and who will execute which parts of the business transaction. It is in these heavily information-based activities that information technologies have some of their most important uses, and it is here that they will have their most profound effects and challenges.

Organizations must begin to manage the evolution of a global information technology architecture that forms an infrastructure for the coordination needs of a global enterprise. A global information system should be a distributed information processing system that crosses national boundaries to support multinational and global enterprises. These global information systems are required to support both flexibility in and coordination among a firm's diverse activities in the new international markets. Widespread industry protocols and standards play key roles in permitting global firms to leverage their systems design and development investments. Although telecommunications standards vary widely from one country to another in terms of the technical details of connecting equipment, and agreements on formats and procedures, conversion of the world's telecommunications facilities into an integrated digital network is ongoing. The challenge is not one of technology, which already exists; rather, integration depends on creating—and interfacing—all components of the information system to deliver seamless services to the end-users no matter in which country.

The telecosmic shift of the global corporations from information access to information analysis and service delivery will significantly change the way information systems and technology are architected in the future. The shift from the importance of hardware to software in the computer/telecommunications industry has accelerated the emergence of a variety of diverse information technologies: multimedia, videoconferencing, mobile computers, and wireless communication devices. The structure of the information technology industry to come is certain to reflect competitors who achieve and expand their core competence in such major areas as software, networks, customer solutions, and service delivery. Information technology contributes to the development and expansion of core competencies and expertise in several ways. Relational databases enable an organization to cumulatively build knowledge bases for creating, nurturing, and maintaining core competencies. Multimedia workstations and just-in-time process-based technology facilitates the renewal and growth of expertise upon which core competencies are developed and used as a competitive weapon for the enterprises. Global information systems enable workers to share knowledge relevant to developing and utilizing the core competencies of the enterprise.

The information and telecommunications technology architecture supports all of the functions and services that an enterprise has to offer. It is imperative to clearly articulate methods and processes to select information technology resources useful to the enterprise, determine their location and management, and shape their development and sourcing. It is this technology architecture that supports the generation, storage, and transmission of knowledge; it forms a framework for the superordinate design of core competencies and expertise, shared knowledge and databases, human assets and structural contours, project tasking and team assignment methodologies, performance measurement, and resource allocation.

Problems Facing the Information Industry

Today, many organizations find themselves dependent upon a diverse collection of hardware platforms, and both standard and custom-developed software applications. These resources may span the globe to support international offices, as well as all fundamental business functions from marketing to research and development, to manufacturing, to accounts receivable. An organization's fundamental capability to conduct its business depends upon the reliable operation of these information systems. Such all-encompassing networks of computing resources are referred to as *enterprise networks* because the operation of an entire organization depends upon them.

The effective management of enterprise networks is a new and potentially daunting challenge. An enterprise network can consist of numerous local area networks (LANs) and wide area networks (WANs), contemporary standards-based systems, and proprietary and legacy systems, all connected by a variety of telecommunications systems (such as satellites and virtual private networks). Most organizations do not have the funds required to replace their proprietary and legacy systems in order to upgrade their management capabilities. They must manage all of their assets concurrently in order to optimize the use of their information management systems. Therefore, real world enterprise information networked systems management solutions must view the whole enterprise as an entity, and encompass both proprietary and legacy systems, as well as the newer systems that conform to current standards. This view of the whole enterprise as an entity is illustrated in Figure 1.1.

Figure 1.1
Leveraging Network-Centric Computing to Enhance Business Value

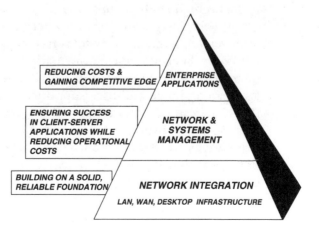

Investments in new networked systems management technology should be justified by increased management staff productivity, increased network reliability, availability and serviceability, and above all better control over a mission-critical infrastructure of the business. Since about 85 percent of enterprises are network dependent, and as a result of increasing cost pressures (in terms of both capital and support), corporate networks are increasingly likely to be synthesized by linking independent departmental and workgroup fiefdoms, or domains. If every group with a network budget can establish management priorities within its domain, the ultimate success of enterprise management, and of enterprise networks, will depend on how well those domains can cooperate.

Information Management: A Business Imperative

In justifying investments in managing enterprise information networks and systems, the first task is understanding a company's motivation. What are the business reasons for companies to integrate and manage their networks and systems? The reasons usually vary. Some companies are downsizing. As a result, they are trying to reduce operating expenses and reallocate staff. Networking and systems support staff, which tend to be viewed as an overhead expense, generally are downsized first. With less staff, companies are hard-pressed to maintain high levels of availability and customer service. Network consolidation and integration simplifies the environment in which these corporations operate and allows them to maintain high levels of support with less staff.

Network integration can also help companies whose adoption of multivendor, stand-alone systems has increased the complexity of their networks. Such complex information networks usually lead to an increase in staff, a decrease in network availability and reliability, and less-than-desirable end-user support. For many corporations, acquisitions have caused explosive growth in the size and complexity of their information networks. This is particularly common among companies that have globalized in recent years. A major drawback in the information network management strategy is that the budget is usually underestimated because the components of end-to-end management of the enterprise's information movement and management needs are incompletely understood.

The information network concerns of global firms involve analyses of how similar or linked activities are performed in different countries. Global information networks are used to manage the exchange of information, goods, expertise, technology, and finances. Corporations are investing a significant amount of their resources to allow the many business functions that play a role in coordination—logistics, order fulfillment, finance, and so forth—to share information about the activities within the firm's value chain.

Although many global firms have an explicit global business strategy, few have a corresponding strategy for managing information networks internationally. Many firms have network interchange protocols across their geographically distributed organizations, but few have a whole system information network management architecture. A global information network management strategy is a necessary response to industry globalization (for example, the growing globalization trend in many industries and the associated dependence on information networks for coordination and operation).

Managing across corporate boundaries has much in common with managing across national borders. Managing a global information network requires one to gather, exchange, and process large volumes of information. Formal strategies and structures cannot support such management information processing needs. Given the widespread distribution of organizational units and the relative infrequency of direct contacts among those in disparate units in a multinational firm, top management has a better opportunity to shape relationships among managers simply by being able to influence the nature and frequency of contacts among them using an appropriate information network management strategy.

An enterprise's information management strategy should include senior management policy on the corporate information network architecture that guides systems development, facilitates integration and data sharing among applications, and supports the development of integrated, corporate systems based on an enterprise-wide data resource. Through appropriate IT design, this strategy must also address organizational and structural issues related to the coordination and configuration of value-chain activities. Some linchpin enablers are a centralized and/or coordinated business/technology strategy for establishing data communications architecture and standards, a centralized and/or coordinated data management strategy for creating corporate databases (data warehouses), and an alignment of business functions and information network management strategies.

It turns out that users want from information network management the same two key factors that the carriers have incorporated into the telecommunications management network (TMN) standards: flexible partitioning of management control with support for boundary cooperation among the network partitions' owners, and the creation of virtual views of services across those boundaries.

The Need for Managing Information Networks

Managing information networks is identified as a requirement in over 95 percent of all network infrastructure and technology architecture and designs, yet research suggests that only one out of eight management-enabled components are actually managed. More networking equipment, systems, and services are being bought and managed at lower levels of the corporate hierarchy. This has resulted in a tremendous drain on the enterprises' resources (both financial and human). These trends have led to the creation of different kinds of networks and, more importantly, have challenged the image of network and systems management as envisioned by the traditional centralized controlling elite.

According to several analysts and industry surveys, a typical organization's information networked systems (INS) expenditure consists of 15 to 20 percent of capital investment; the rest is support and management costs. This suggests that about 80 percent of IT costs are overhead for a corporation. It is a challenging time of transition as enterprises enter the distributed computing age and attempt to shed the centralized, tightly coupled organization and architectures. At a time when nearly every organization is buying network components, the various business units need only a simplified or limited view of each other's networks.

With the increasing importance of controlling costs and "glocal" (view globally, act locally!) importance of managing global information networks, many vendors of LAN and WAN network management systems have been adding management of more device types and wider internetworking capabilities, and then proudly proclaiming their systems as integrated or enterprise. A major challenge facing global corporations today is the need to align business strategy and structure with information networks management and development strategy. Appropriate design of critical linkages among a firm's value-chain activities results in an effective business design involving information technology and improved coordination with coalition partners as well as among the corporation's own subsidiaries.

Managing global information networks requires more than mere technical capabilities. The ability to operate effectively with multinational cultures, sensitivity to the demands and intrigues of top management, and a comprehensive view of business processes are examples of the skills needed internationally within the systems development functions. Many IT managers do not understand how IT can transform operations globally. This is usually due to their myopic view of managing information networks involving only technology and nothing else. Because they were not designed to be cross-functional, much less cross-national, their entrenched, nonintegrated business processes and systems naturally resist a management system for a global information network. Moreover, old systems carry the baggage of diverse technology and incompatible management applications, making it even more difficult to build common global information network management systems.

Today, end-users like virtual structures because they let each independent domain within an enterprise network segregate the facilities or resources that meet its internal needs from the needs of the enterprise as a whole. Each domain's devices are, in general, dedicated to its internal users, but some also provide connectivity to the rest of the enterprise (especially in the age of the internet). A more modern view says the other domains should be concerned only with the state of the service agreement these devices support and the owning organization has committed to provide.

All of these challenges make a better catalyst to further drain the resources of enterprises that are merely surviving without adding any value to their shareholders. Hence, it is imperative to develop a clear strategy for managing the global information network and its associated components.

CHAPTER 2

Management Standards

Introduction

Network and systems management standards are constantly evolving and undergoing dramatic changes. The status of several standard documents is being elevated, and addenda are being created to formalize and finalize standards. A method has been established for amending standards to reflect feedback from actual experience, and certain common network management functional areas have been identified.

The objective of this chapter is to help the reader gain a general understanding of the standards as related to networking management and as defined by International Standards Organization (ISO), internet, and Institute of Electrical and Electronics Engineers (IEEE) network management standards. It is important to understand the various protocols and standards as these will be referred to later in the book as it delves into the design of an integrated network and systems management strategy. (*Some of the standards and protocols are discussed more for historical perspective than for current trends or practices.*) Readers who require in-depth understanding of the standards discussed in this book are referred to the various reference publications cited in the bibliography.

The networking management industry is carefully following the progress of OSI management standards. There are differing schools of thought on this subject matter: Is OSI management the ultimate network management solution, is it just an academic's dream, or is it a bottleneck for the industry? The answer lies somewhere in between.

OSI Management Framework

The OSI management framework provides the concepts and definitions for OSI management (both systems and network). It also introduces the five broad functional components of OSI management: fault, performance, security, configuration, and accounting. In addition, it explains the concepts of individual layer management, and the concepts of managed objects and object manager. Figure 2.1 details the OSI Network Management Related Standards. One might ask why we need an object oriented model. The answer is that object orientation is specifically designed for managing complexity—the only real limitation faced in networking today. Today's networking technology has just about overcome the limitations of bandwidth and memory. High-performance workstations, client/server technology, and PCs are commonplace, and are relatively inexpensive to connect. This combination of factors has fostered an explosive growth of networks, and a looming headache of how to manage them.

What Is Object Orientation?

Object orientation breaks down into small pieces ("objects") the problem of managing complexity. Thus, an object-oriented model looks at the network piece by piece instead of viewing it in its overwhelmingly complex entirety. Each individual piece, (e.g., element, software module, or logical component) is modeled separately, so it is easier to understand. Furthermore, the concept of inheritance allows classes of individual models to be copied and applied to model similar devices. This saves a lot of effort in constructing the entire, composite enterprise network model. The various advantages will be clearly evident in later chapters.

OSI Management Framework Standards

The consideration of networking management within the OSI context is purely a consideration within a "standards" context. The relevant question

Figure 2.1
Network Manage-
ment Related Stan-
dards - OSI

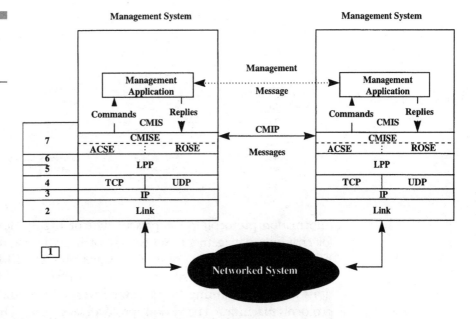

Figure 2.1
Network Management Related Standards - OSI

is, "What must be standardized in order to affect network management?" The answer is, quite simply, the two broad elements of network management: the definition of management information and the ability to move management information throughout the network. The processing of management information is considered a local issue and is not subject to standardization (within these contexts). It will, in fact, be one element that network management system providers and vendors will use to differentiate their OSI products from those of other manufacturers. In addition, OSI does not standardize network management policies, what to do with management information, storage and access mechanism of management information, and user interface.

The framework providing the big overview for OSI network management is depicted in Figure 2.2. At the top of the tree is the director whose objectives are to understand the logical and physical scope of the network, to be able to control each part of the network directly or indirectly, to provide security across the system, and to administer the network properly. Distributed throughout the network are the computers, communications switches, routers, and gateways that enable the network to operate. From this very general network structure comes the overall framework for OSI network management.

Over the past few years, the OSI network management definitions have progressed from the original concept of CMIP (control and management

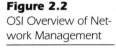

Figure 2.2
OSI Overview of Network Management

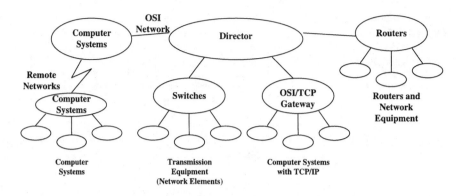

information protocol) to the present state of highly flexible architecture for enabling management and control of large diverse network elements. Within the OSI framework, the managed objects will be objects whose definition is the responsibility of OSI standards (i.e., data communications objects pertaining to the seven layers of OSI and their associated protocols machines). The various protocol layer groups have been charged with defining the managed objects for the layers for which they are responsible. The ability to move management information throughout the network is accomplished by the OSI CMIP (common management information protocol) and supporting protocols. CMIP is an application layer protocol; its supporting services include ACSE (association control service element), ROSE (remote operations service element), presentation, and the rest of the OSI stack.

OSI Management Architecture

The OSI management architecture can be decomposed into four main subdivisions: environment, structure, services, and protocols. A brief discussion of each of these subdivisions follows.

Environment. The OSI management environment is concerned with the tools and services needed to control and supervise managed network objects and their interconnection activities. The environment itself could be categorized into three models:

■ Organizational Model: this describes the ways network management can be distributed administratively across management domains and the ways management systems can be distributed within a domain. The organizational model contains a recursive property. Figure 2.3 illustrates the organizational model.

Figure 2.3
OSI Organization
Model

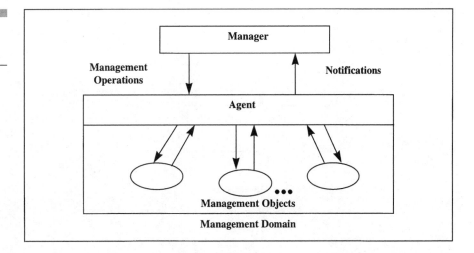

Figure 2.3
OSI Organization
Model

- Informational Model: this provides the manner in which managed objects are defined. An object definition includes its class, attributes, actions, name, and interrelationships with other objects. In effect, it provides guidelines for describing the logical structure of the managed objects and other pertinent management information about such objects. This is depicted in Figure 2.4.

- Functional Model: this defines those functions provided by the environment to achieve the user requirements. These functions are performed either locally or remotely via communication among the open systems or by real-time virtual connections. The five major functional areas are fault, performance, security, configuration, and accounting. The functional model is illustrated in Figures 2.5, 2.6, 2.7, 2.8, and 2.9.

Figure 2.4
OSI Information
Model

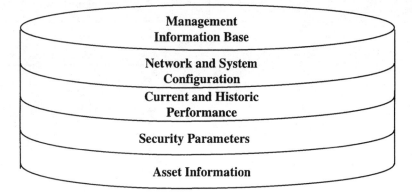

Figure 2.5
OSI Functional Model
- Fault Management

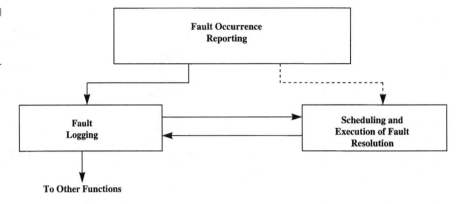

Figure 2.6
OSI Functional Model
- Configuration Man-
agement

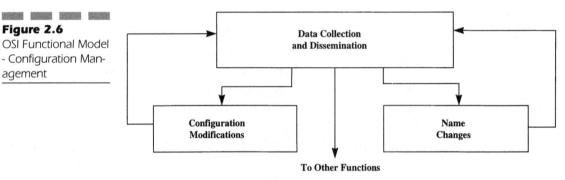

Figure 2.7
OSI Functional Model
- Configuration Man-
agement

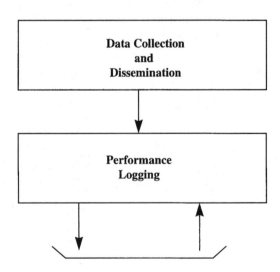

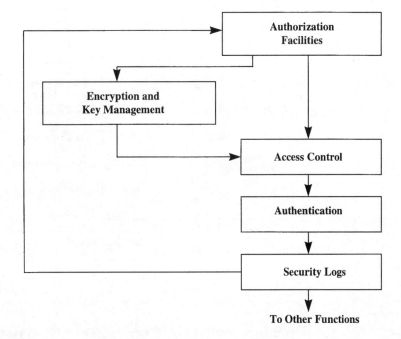

Figure 2.8
OSI Functional Model
- Security Management

Structure. The OSI management structure is based on and overlaid onto the ISO OSI seven-layer reference model. The systems management applications (SMA) process can execute both local and remote systems management functions. This service is achieved via the systems management interface (SMI). The management information base (MIB) represents the repository of information for the SMA process. An indirect means of communication between the SMA process and any one of the seven layers is also available by the MIB. The OSI structure definition is depicted in Figure 2.10

Services. The OSI management services, previously termed common management and information services (CMIS), represent the backbone of the

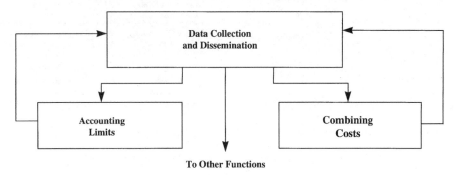

Figure 2.9
OSI Functional Model
- Accounting Management

Figure 2.10
OSI Management
Structure Definition

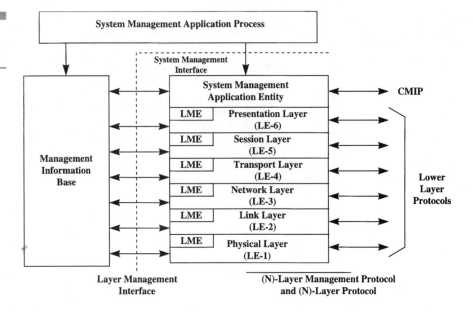

five functional areas. Three categories of services exist: event (and data) reporting, data manipulation, and control. These services are provided by the common management and information services element (CMISE). Some examples as related to the OSI management services are depicted in Figure 2.11.

Figure 2.11
OSI Management
Services

Management Functional Areas	Common Management and Information Services		
	Event Reporting	Data Manipulation	Control
Fault	Occurrence Reporting	Fault Logging	Scheduling and Execution
Configuration and Name	Object Creation Reports, Attribute Change Reports	Modifications Data Collection and Dissemination	Changes
Performance	Workload Monitoring, Measurement Summaries	Data Collection and Dissemination, Performance Logging	
Accounting	Accounting Records	Data Collection and Dissemination, Audit Functions	
Security	Authentication, Security Logs	Security Logs	Access Control, Authentication
Other	Event Forwarding, Control Discrimination	Logging (General)	Discrimination Criteria

Figure 2.12
OSI Management
Information
Exchange Protocols

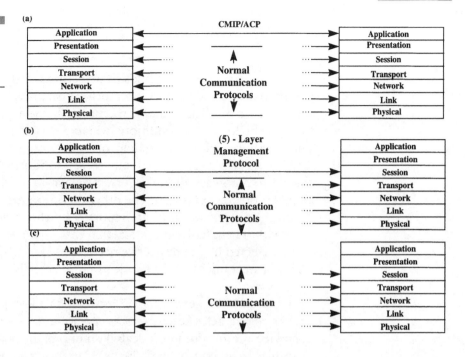

Protocols. Three main types of protocols assist in achieving network management functions: common management information protocol (CMIP), (N)-layer management protocol, and (N)-protocol. For systems management, CMIP is utilized at layer seven in addition to its use in peer-to-peer communication between SMAEs. Management at a specific layer is accomplished by (N)-layer management protocol, which embodies more management functionality than an (N)-protocol. An (N)-protocol represents the normal end-user communication. The OSI management information exchange protocols are illustrated in Figure 2.12.

OSI Network Management Functional Areas

Networking management includes five functional areas: fault management, performance management, security management, configuration and name management, and accounting management. Each of these areas will be discussed briefly.

Fault Management. Fault management (FM) is concerned with the detection, isolation, and correction of network problems as they occur, or any irregularities in network performance. FM is closely related to performance and configuration management because when performance of a network degrades or when a fault occurs, the network manager very often has to reconfigure one or several portions of the network, move users or resources, or procure additional bandwidth.

There are two distinct methods of detecting faults: proactive and reactive. Proactive detection uses a monitoring system like a network element manager that periodically checks the network and its health. This monitoring system looks for conditions where a problem is building (e.g., a queue length exceeding a threshold, or traffic congestion) but a fault has not yet necessarily occurred. Usually these monitoring systems also have provision to automatically take corrective action in response to certain potential problem conditions. The other detection method in FM is reactive. Some problems or faults are reported by the various subsystems of the network. These faults are in reaction to a problem after an error condition is detected by the respective network element. In effect, FM tells us what is not working in the network, given the configuration.

Performance Management.   Performance management (PM) deals with the function that helps keep networks operating at the service level users expect and require. In addition, it deals with improving network performance on a regular basis for a network manager to meet the predefined network performance objectives and the service level users expect and require. PM is closely related to proactive fault management. In both cases, performance thresholds are established and the network is monitored for any deviations from these thresholds. When a deviation is detected, the network manager switches to fault management mode (corrective action) before the network condition deteriorates. In effect, PM tells us how the network is behaving and performing against its potential.

Security Management.   Security management (SM) is the process of controlling network access and protecting network objects. A database is defined to maintain a record of the network privileges for each user. This includes access to hosts, or read and write privileges for individual files on a file server. SM also includes provisions for encryption and user authentication. SM provides tools for the system administrator to manage a geographically and functionally dispersed network.

Configuration Management.   Configuration management (CM) includes name management, inventory management, and directory services. This function identifies, administers, and controls systems objects for the purpose of providing continuous operation of the network. This is done through the management of the characteristics of network objects such as routing tables, port addresses, and different protocols. Name management is particularly important in an integrated WAN environment. Symbolic names used in this environment allow the users to access hosts, applications, and databases without having to know where they reside on the network. Management of the symbolic names is critical for keeping track of changes in network resources. Inventory management is the maintenance of historical and financial information regarding network equipment. In effect, CM tells us where everything in the network is, how it is interconnected, and what the operating parameters are for each element.

Accounting Management. Accounting management (AM) deals with tracking and allocating network resources and costs according to the needs and objectives of the user. It also addresses placing limits on the use of managed objects and elements, and informs users of costs incurred or resources consumed. AM is more important in WANs since the users are typically charged by network usage.

OSI Network Management Components

The system management application entity (SMAE) contains the OSI application layer communication components required for network management. The SMAE is a required component on each and every system within the OSI management environment. Within the SMAE are the SMASE, CMISE, and ACSE/ROSE. The SMAE uses an OSI stack to communicate with other open systems. This stack includes the OSI presentation, session, and transport layers. Above the SMAE is the application process (AP). This component contains the agent and/or manager functionality necessary to provide a managed and/or manager system. The various OSI network management components are depicted in Figure 2.13.

As discussed earlier, in OSI management, hardware and software are viewed and managed in terms of objects. The CMISE provides a transaction type of service necessary for sending and receiving messages to/from remote systems. Contained within this element are the CMIP and the associated service (CMIS). These components provide the protocol and service necessary to support CMISE capabilities. CMISE uses the services of ACSE and ROSE. ACSE provides the means of establishing a management association between peer SMAEs for the purpose of exchanging management information. ROSE is used to invoke remote operations on these remote systems.

Figure 2.13
OSI Network Management Components

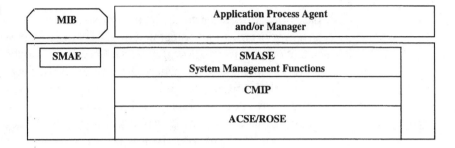

Internet Management Framework

A large number of installations use the transmission control protocol/ internet protocol (TCP/IP) in their LANs and WANs. These protocols were developed within the internet framework and are used extensively throughout the world. Because of its very wide use, the standards relating to management of internets is gaining enormous importance. In addition, one other reason for its popularity is the limited availability of OSI management standards-based products and services. In recognition of this fact, the Internet Activities Board (IAB) has assumed the lead in setting standards for TCP/IP based internets and has sponsored two network management protocols. One protocol, which is intended to address short-term solutions, is called the simple network management protocol (SNMP). The other protocol, which proposes to address long-range solutions, is called common management information services and protocol over TCP/IP (CMOT). This standard is rarely used in today's environment.

Internet uses the term *network element* to describe any object that is managed. This term means the same as *OSI-managed object*. The internet network management standards are designed to allow the communication of management information between agents located in the network elements and a network management control center. Figure 2.14 illustrates

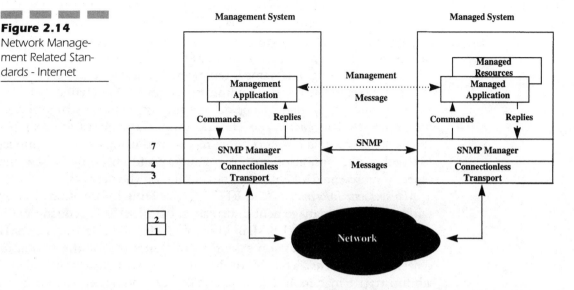

Figure 2.14
Network Management Related Standards - Internet

the managed element/system consisting of the SNMP agent, the SNMP manager, and the managed objects and resources.

The current internet management framework is based on three components:

- the internet-standard SMI
- the internet-standard MIB
- the SNMP

The terms SMI and MIB are similar to the ones used in the OSI management framework. However, the use and scope of these terms in the internet management framework are somewhat different.

Internet Management Standards

Request for comment (RFC) is the internet equivalent to formal standards. This section will describe only the standards (or components) that are applicable to our discussion. The reader is advised to refer to complete RFCs for more extensive coverage of the relevant topics.

Structure of Management Information: RFC 1155 contains common definitions and identification of information used on TCP/IP-based networks. It is similar in intent to the OSI Network Management Standard IS 7498-4 and IS 10040.

Managed objects are accessed via a virtual information store, defined as the MIB. Objects in the MIB are defined using abstract syntax notation one (ASN.1). Each type of object (termed an object type) has a name, a syntax, and an encoding. The name is represented uniquely as an object identifier. An object identifier is an administratively assigned name.

The syntax for an object type defines the abstract data structure corresponding to that object type. The encoding of an object type is simply how instances of that object type are represented using its syntax. Implicitly tied to the notion of an object's syntax and encoding is how the object is represented when being transmitted on the network.

Management Information Base. RFC 1213 contains information dealing with an internet management information base (IMIB). This document is the second release of the MIB, known as MIB II. The internet SMI describes the identification scheme and structure for the managed objects in an internet. The SMI deals principally with organizational and administrative matters. It leaves the task of class and object definitions to the other network management related RFCs.

The MIB consists of a set of managed objects and their attributes. The MIB is used by the system management entities in the application layer to communicate with each other and with the (N)-layer management entities. The idea of the MIB is to link systems management, layer management, and layer operations together.

The objects within an internet have several common characteristic across subnetworks, vendor products, and individual components. The IMIB provides a registration scheme wherein objects can be defined and categorized within a registration hierarchy. The internet network management structure is organized around object groups. Each of these object groups is discussed in detail in RFC 1213.

Simple Network Management Protocol.   SNMP provides management applications with a simple set of commands that are packaged using the basic encoding rules (BER) associated with ISO ASN.1 and sent over existing UDP/IP services. There is also a trap message, which allows standardized types of unconfirmed events to be reported asynchronously. Implicit in the SNMP architectural model is a collection of network management stations and network elements. Network management stations execute management applications that monitor and control network elements. Network elements are devices such as hosts, gateways, terminal servers, and the like, which have management agents responsible for performing the network management functions requested by the network management stations. SNMP is used to communicate management information between the stations and the agents.

Figure 2.15
SNMP Architecture

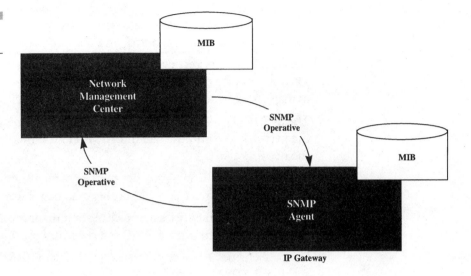

Figure 2.15 shows the SNMP architecture that articulates a solution to the network management problem in terms of the following:

- the scope of the management information communicated by the protocol,

- the representation of the management information communicated by the protocol,

- operations on management information supported by the protocol,

- the form and meaning of exchanges among management entities,

- the definition of administrative relationships among management entities, and

- the form and meaning of references to management information.

The SNMP processes must occur either in managed entities or in an associated proxy server. For example, a router must have built-in software acting as an SNMP agent. Two sets of logical processes occur within those managed elements: the relationships that are specified between various network management entities, and the way network management information is communicated.

The SNMP standard, RFC 1157, and the SNMP administrative model, RFC 1351, define a number of terms and describe relationships between different components associated with the overall network management model:

- Network management servers are systems that execute the management applications that monitor, control, and manage the network elements.

- Network elements are devices such as hosts, bridges, routers, hubs, and software systems that contain an agent and perform the network management functions that the management server requests.

- The SNMP allows management servers and the agents (or proxies) in the network to communicate information associated with managing the network itself.

- The SNMP proxy agent provides management functions on behalf of network elements that would otherwise be inaccessible.

- SNMP application entities reside either at a management station or at a managed node, and use SNMP as a communication mechanism.

- Protocol entities are peer processes that implement SNMP, thus supporting the SNMP application entities.

- The SNMP community pairs an SNMP agent with an arbitrary set of SNMP application entities. The administrator assigns the community a name (called the community name), which is essentially a password with associated rights and privileges. A management application with multiple community names may belong to multiple communities.

- Authentic SNMP messages are SNMP messages sent from an application entity to a specific SNMP community. The message contains the community name of interest.

- The authentication scheme is the method by which an SNMP message is identified as belonging to a specific SNMP community.

- The MIB view is the subset of MIB objects, which may be contained within several subtrees that pertain to a network element.

- The SNMP access mode determines the level of access to objects that a particular application entity is allowed.

- The community profile pairs the SNMP access mode with the SNMP MIB view. The community profile represents specific access privileges for the variables in a MIB view.

- The SNMP access policy pairs an SNMP community with an SNMP community profile. The access policy represents the specific community profile that an agent permits the other members of the community to have.

More details on these aspects can be found in the various literature describing SNMP or the RFCs themselves (see bibliography).

A fundamental concept that should be clear in either OSI or internet management is that, in either case, the overall networked system environment to be managed is being segmented into smaller manageable entities (managed objects) and certain attributes (MIB) are associated with those objects. Further, a broad class of objects are defined for any network and the composite network consists of several instances of those classes of objects. This is the main idea behind open network management systems.

Managed objects are accessed via a virtual information store, termed the MIB. Objects in the MIB are defined using ASN.1. Designers need not worry about learning the ASN.1 syntax as there are several commercially available tools to develop the MIB using either graphical language or fourth-generation language. The virtual information store is organized conceptually as a tree with named edges (or arcs or branches). The objects are at the leaves of the tree. The entire path from the root through the tree to the object identifies the object. Each object has a class name and instance as described above, and the class name information and instance information are concatenated together to yield the complete object name.

The SNMP message itself is divided into two sections: a version identifier plus community name, and a protocol data unit (PDU). The version identifier and community name are sometimes referred to as the SNMP authentication header. There are five different PDU types: GetRequest, GetNextRequest, GetResponse, SetRequest, and Trap. The Get, Set, and Response PDUs have a common format, while the Trap PDU format is unique. The version number assures that both the management server and the agent are using the same version of the SNMP protocol. The community name authenticates the manager before allowing access to the agent.

The Trap PDU is a powerful operative to design effective standard network management systems. Often this is not given too much attention. But, in this book, Trap is used extensively to address the management-by-exception approach undertaken to architect an integrated management system for distributed services network. The agent (or the proxy) uses the Trap PDU to alert the manager that a predefined event has occurred. Traps are application specific and RFC 1215 offers some guidance for defining Traps for use with the SNMP standards.

As described earlier, SNMP proxy agents are becoming popular for several reasons: shielding other agents from redundant network management requests and answering from cached information; providing instrumentation via translation for non-IP or non-SNMP entities; and agent multiplexing to attain multiple agents per managed system. In some cases, multiple management stations (or even multiple management processes on the same station) require access to the same information on a repetitive basis. A proxy daemon may be used to shield the agents from redundant network management requests and respond cached information. It is a nontrivial task to walk a sparse table with confidence using Get-Nexts and cached information.

Proxy engines may be used to permit the monitoring and control of network elements otherwise not addressable using the management protocol and transport protocol. There is no difference between a regular agent and a proxy agent. However, some vendors provide sophisticated features, such as event filters, provision for thresholding, and so forth, along with the proxy agent. These features are extremely useful, as will become obvious later in the book, in developing a standard networking management strategy for networks consisting of non-SNMP devices.

SNMP has certain limitations and hence the new version of SNMP (SNMP version two or SNMPv2) that is emerging as a standard and should address several of the limitations of SNMP version 1. SNMPv2 will be used in agents, in management servers, in manager-to-manager applications, and in several management applications. SNMPv2 is very useful in both systems and applications management. SNMPv2 was developed based on careful consideration of identified perceived defects, building on a successful existing base, and backward compatible whenever possible. Some key highlights of SNMPv2 are:

- a few new data types
- improved efficiency through new bulk retrieval mechanism (GetBulk)
- improved sets, especially row creation and deletion
- richer error return values for exception handling
- new support for manager-to-manager communications
- tightened language to eliminate ambiguities, avoid frequent errors, and address frequently asked questions
- it uses the already done work on SNMP security
- TCP/IP-centric aspects removed to be more compatible with types of networks

The SNMPv2 message formats define two independent components for SNMP packets: message wrapper and PDU. These new proposals redefine the message wrapper without modifying the syntax or semantics of the protocol data units. SNMPv2 offers additional security features such as codifying MIB views, further defining proxy naming, and offering support for non TCP/IP networks.

IEEE Management Standards

The reason for a brief discussion on IEEE management standards and protocols will be clear in later chapters as we discuss various types of network services, including LANs and WANs. Several of the IEEE standards are adopted from ISO standards themselves. The approach taken by the IEEE in their LAN and metropolitan area network (LAN/MAN) management standards is to implement a network management protocol at the lower two layers of the OSI model. This is primarily due to the fact that the IEEE standards are typically two-layer standard. The approach taken by IEEE is referred to as CMIP (OSI standard) over logical link layer (LLC), or CMOL.

Network management at layers 1 and 2 of a LAN typically focuses on detecting, isolating, and diagnosing faults. Several types of devices support these network areas. LAN network management is obviously of greater importance when the LAN becomes large and complex. As companies create their own LAN internetworks by linking workgroup LANs, they create a need for LAN network management, and interest in LAN management standards and architectures. With the advent of client/server architectures and computing, LAN management becomes even more important, adding LAN network management to the multiplicity of management domains. In today's world, most applications adopt a simple paradigm of having the host system manage LAN applications. This will involve direct LAN-to-HOST connectivity, including the distribution of software components of such LAN applications.

SUMMARY

Those who follow the formal standards process will relate this need to the OSI management model, with its set of CCITT X.700 standards, including the CMIP and the CMIS. Implementation of an early version of these standards was defined by the Network Management Forum (NMF), a consortium of vendors and users trying to promote a common approach to network and systems management.

Those who follow the computing consortium's work will note a close correlation between the management needs and the Open Software Foundation's (OSF) work. OSF is a vendor-dominated open systems group that is developing a software platform to support distributed management applications, known as the distributed management environment (DME). This standard is rarely used in today's environment.

Another computing consortium, the Object Management Group (OMG), is focusing on object-oriented technology and has defined the common object request broker architecture as a way to achieve the benefits of object-oriented design in real products.

The challenge to the network management industry is to make all of these related pieces fit neatly together. These groups and others are working together under an umbrella called OMNIPoint. The idea behind OMNIPoint is to harness the many activities under way in each of several key consortia, to factor in progress towards formal standards, and to create a useful link to de facto standards. The result is a stake in the ground that provides stability in a rapidly changing world, allowing customers and suppliers to invest in technology safely.

CHAPTER 3

Information Networks

Introduction

In the forefront of the transition of a firm to a globally coordinated and managed organization is information network. Information networks can drive the change, be harnessed to it, or rise up as a severe impediment. The integration of information technology and telecommunications, termed *information networking*, is having a significant impact on the structure of industries, on the competitive strategies of firms in these industries, and on the way firms cooperate within and across industries. Information networking can drive a company towards globalization in a number of ways. Using computer and communications technologies, firms can extract the information components from tangible products, or substitute knowledge for material, and then instantly transport the electronically represented information or knowledge throughout the world.

In many cases, IT networking is changing the very fabric of how firms perform their core activities. In attempting to gain or enhance their competitive advantage, firms are making extraordinary investments in IT networking and its management without being entirely sure of how these investments will ultimately pay off, or how they will be deployed global-ly and organization-wide. In this chapter we investigate the necessary strategies that are essential for a whole system architecture for managing the information networking infrastructure. Further, this chapter will dis-cuss how global business drivers dictate that the most important pre-scription for successful global implementation of business application is a shared common management data model. Commonality in the hardware, systems software, and organizational structure are secondary concerns. Both the technology architecture and the organization's structure can accommodate some amount of international variability as long as (a) management data can be successfully passed from node to node in a communication network, (b) there is shared meaning of data, and (c) an organization-wide agreement exists as to how management work is to be allocated among different business units. A side benefit of this approach is that it provides significant opportunities to achieve economies of scale within the systems functions by instituting a more standardized approach to managing hardware, software, and networking infrastructure.

Whole System Architecture

Global information networking systems are by nature distributed. Dis-tributed systems management, along with a need to be more service ori-ented, are driving organizations to pursue process-driven (versus technol-ogy-driven) organizational structures for shared infrastructure manage-ment. Two significant trends—the shift towards distributed networked computing (client/server, internet, and intranet) and the repositioning of IT as an internal service provider—are driving organizations to move from a traditional technology-centric structure and architecture to a more process-oriented model.

Client/server computing is changing the way IT organizations need to approach information network management. In the mainframe world, applications are contained within the data center and all logic for a par-ticular application typically runs on a single process. Therefore, it is possi-ble to draw lines between different technology layers (hardware, software, networking, desktop) that make up the infrastructure, and establish orga-nizational entities responsible for the life-cycle management of each layer. However, as IT organizations shift their focus towards distributed systems and applications, business transactions and applications span the entire information infrastructure—from desktop to central computer center, irrespective of their location and stored format. Thus, to manage how well the infrastructure meets application requirements (performance, availability, scalability, accessibility, etc.), there is a need for a single, integrated operations management organization responsible for the end-to-end infrastructure. However, this organization may not be the controller of the network but instead may be the coordinator of the activities and processes. The interdependencies of distributed computing technology also create a need to pool systems integration resources into project teams that can be leveraged across the enterprise.

The role of IT organizations is changing by the day. The spending budgets of IT departments are questioned on a regular basis and are being tied to such metrics as economic value added to the corporation, return on investment, and shareholder satisfaction. Hence they are becoming more service oriented and customer centric and less technology driven. In addition, several enterprises are outsourcing part or all of their IT management activities. This phenomenon is further accentuated by the repositioning of IT as an internal vendor of services, required to market and sell its services internally, often in competition with outside service providers and outsourcers. If corporations are to succeed in managing their global information networks under this new business model, they must treat networking management as a business imperative and run it like a business rather than delegating it to some local technicians.

The most important architectural strategy is simply to have a comprehensive whole system architecture for managing global information networks. The problem would be utterly intractable without an architectural framework. A generic framework for managing a globally distributed information network is described in Figure 3-1.

Cost and Benefit Analysis

Traditional ROI calculations are not adequate to justify spending on networking management infrastructure. New approaches that tie benefits more directly to business applications are needed. The significant shift towards value-based pricing (and activity-based costing and management) for both IT and IT management services will require more robust management techniques.

It has proven particularly difficult to carry out ROI analyses for networking management investments. Given the fundamental positioning of associated services among IT's overall task portfolio, the inability to

Figure 3.1

Framework for Managing Globally Distributed Information Networks

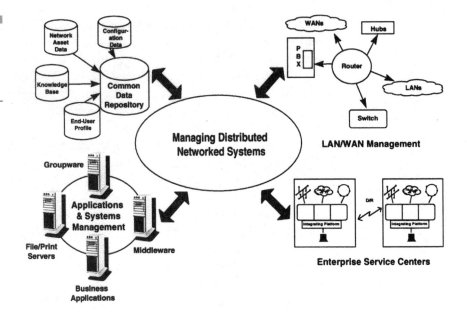

execute such justifications will severely hamper internal IT's effectiveness and threaten its survival. Some of the difficulty stems from the uncertainty surrounding any attempt to project networking management costs and benefits, but the core problem involves determining just what things count as networking infrastructure costs or benefits. At the same time major corporations are increasingly unwilling to treat networking management spending and budgets as necessary and, in the interests of cost reduction, are demanding even more granular accounts even of small infrastructural investments.

Today, most companies' ROI analysis for investments in networking management still involves a net present value (NPV) calculation. The life cycle of a project investment is broken down into discreet time periods. The expected value of the benefits for each period is calculated (the expected value being the average of the benefits accruing from the investment according to different possible scenarios, weighted by the anticipated probabilities associated with each of those scenarios) and then discounted according to an appropriate interest rate. Finally, the present value of the costs is subtracted from the present value of the benefits, with a positive balance suggesting that the investment should be made and a negative balance suggesting that the investment should be foregone.

It is rarely simple to figure out what precisely constitutes the costs or the benefits. Traditionally, costs have been calculated primarily from hardware/software prices using standard depreciation schedules and personnel/support costs, while benefits have been articulated in terms of head-count reduction and somewhat arbitrary determinations of increased productivity or revenue-generating opportunity.

The benefits derived from networking management infrastructure investments have proven particularly hard to capture and present in a manner that makes their case to corporate decision makers. In general, while business application-related investments are justified through their contribution to lines of business (LOBs), networking management investments are too often justified in terms of their impact on operational staffing and budgets. In other words, networking management investments are rarely seen as contributing to the value of an application, but rather as possibly reducing some operations overhead.

Several problems arise with this point of view. First, in the wake of process-driven downsizing and activity-based costing and management, the networking management staff of many companies is already close to minimal. It is unlikely that the introduction of a comparatively expensive software component, accompanied by the requisite systems integration charges, will be justifiable in terms of significant head-count reduction within infrastructure operations departments. Nor will such an investment likely increase the individual productivity of operations staff. Second, in the case of distributed applications, much of the networking management function will be located within the LOB, and consequently its execution will not directly involve central operations staff. The benefits, therefore, cannot be directly tied to cost reductions within the boundaries of central infrastructure management. The net result of these two problems has been an architectural, spending, and organizational chaos caused by different departments managing different pieces of the information network and not taking a systemic approach towards an end-to-end management.

A possible solution to these problems is to find a method of associating networking management infrastructure investment more directly with the value generated by business applications. If such an association can be made, then investment is likely to be more forthcoming, and return on those investments could be substantially tangible.

The first type of value is availability of business applications. If a revenue-generating application cannot be launched or becomes inoperable, then the revenue stream associated with that application will not flow while the application is unavailable. Assuming the LOB knows how to calculate the revenues generated by a business application when it is up and running, it should be possible to estimate the impact that unavailability will have on the revenue stream. The networking management component could be partially justified through its contribution to a given application's availability. For this, the application management has to be an integral part of overall networking management.

The second type of value is performance. Increase in response time generally means that more transactions invoking a given application can be performed. The LOB should be able to calculate the revenues associated with a transaction; hence, an increase in transaction response, leading to an increase in the number of transactions performed, will then lead to measurable increase in revenues generated. These revenues could be associated with a transaction with portions of networking management infrastructure, and consequently could be used to partially justify its implementation.

The third type of value is decrease in support services costs. While it may prove increasingly difficult to reduce general support head count through the implementation of an enterprise networking management, it should nonetheless be possible to demonstrate a reduction in charge-back service time consumed to support a given business application. Furthermore, LOB time spent on administrative and support tasks associated with applications management and maintenance might also be reduced by the introduction of an appropriate networking management component. As both these costs can be effectively allocated to individual applications, their reduction can be used to partially justify an investment in management infrastructure.

With three types of potential value for each application, an investment in networking management can then be justified if the present value of its associated costs is outstripped by the present value of the sum of the benefits it contributes to the entire corporate application portfolio. Hence a fundamental paradigm shift in the way networking management is architected is imperative. No amount of investment in infrastructure management can be justified if the business units do not see any value or an impact on their operations. It is critical and more often essential that the business model, the financial model, and the operating model be embedded in the overall whole system architecture for managing the global information network. More often than not, the information networking management architecture as outlined in Figure 3.1 is not aligned with the overall IT architecture as illustrated in Figure 3.2.

Caveats of the Analysis

While the advantages of cost/benefit analysis and global strategies can be great, there are a few dangers. First, the analysis can be performed at too high a level. *Global impact, global markets, global business drivers,*

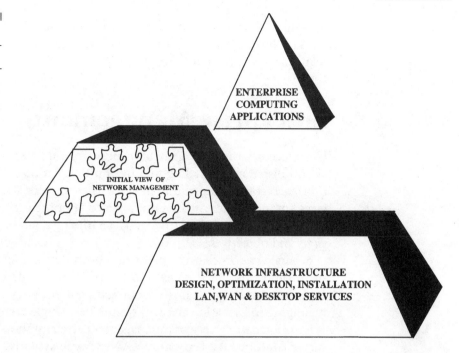

Figure 3.2
Misalignment of Management Systems

ENTERPRISE
COMPUTING
APPLICATIONS

INITIAL VIEW OF
NETWORK MANAGEMENT

NETWORK INFRASTRUCTURE
DESIGN, OPTIMIZATION, INSTALLATION
LAN, WAN & DESKTOP SERVICES

and *revenue erosion* are phrases that can quickly capture corporate decision makers' attention and may be life-and-death concerns for many corporations. But such generalities are far removed from the day-to-day realities of running a business and maintaining a networking infrastructure. The cost/benefit analysis must emphasize the specifics of the business impact and quantifiable costs savings and productivity improvements in addition to direct impact on revenues and earnings.

Another danger in the analysis comes from failing to recognize differences within the firm. Business drivers are seldom exactly the same across business units. Although there may be opportunities to build synergy across businesses, the richest opportunities are at the business unit level.

The third danger is related to cultural differences across business units that may make it difficult to reach consensus initially on the corporate business drivers. Often there are sharp differences across business units, both domestically and globally, in the factors thought to contribute to a firm's success. While some rate customer service as the most important element, some view workforce skills and product development as more significant.

The fourth danger comes from the lack of senior business management involvement in the cost/benefit analysis. Senior management must be willing to sponsor and participate in the cost/benefit analysis and play a leadership role in the move to an integrated information networking management infrastructure.

Enterprise Management

Until recently, the management of networks and systems has been a casual and disparate effort handled by multiple groups within an organization, each controlling and managing its own piece. Multiple support services sprang up across the enterprise to support each link in the chain. They were typically organized by technology rather than by business goals and objectives.

Several vendors claim to be solving both network and systems management problems, but they tend to sell point solutions, unintegrated products operated by vertical, distinct organizations. They miss a major point: managing information networks must be a single architecture. An enterprise information network management strategy should encompass four major components: LAN and WAN devices, systems and applications, a common management information repository, and an enterprise service center. If a company includes these four components in its management strategy, deploying and justifying such infrastructure is easy and convincing. An important ingredient across all these components is service level—the expected response rate to a networking problem or the expected performance of an application.

A Whole New World

Today's separate set of tools for information networking management stems from the evolution of client/server systems. During the mainframe era, the only thing that needed to be managed was the system and its applications. But as the number of local area networks and workgroups proliferated, the technical sophistication both of end-users and of the client/server environment grew, and a generation of tools to manage network components emerged. Corporations began downsizing their computers during the last few years, and many also reduced their staffs, resulting in fewer people to manage the systems and more reliance on systems management products.

To deal with the complexity of today's globally networked client/server environment, network and systems operators must have easy access to configuration, status, and performance information. The enterprise management infrastructure model must be expanded to include every complex resource, including other management systems and management domains. Most managers think that managing the global information networks consists only of managing the systems and network devices. But a more comprehensive approach encompasses tools such as asset management, service-level management, applications management, systems management, desktop equipment management, and network instrumentation, as well as the traditional functions of managing faults, configuration, accounting, performance and security.

Managing a globally distributed information network entails several functions, including analyzing data, isolating faults, reconfiguring the network, taking action prior to service disruption, identifying chronic failures, maintaining agreed service levels, managing and controlling business applications without rewriting them on a regular basis, and gaining maximum use from applications and servers. Because management information is not available across different brands of network and systems management products in common format—many of which deploy different protocols—the above tasks are nearly impossible for managers to perform, and they are equally difficult to automate.

Without a means of gathering management information by using standard protocols and a common data model, no one person or system can truly manage an enterprise's information network. If corporations cannot control their networks today, imagine their predicament in a few years when an explosion in internet computing and personal digital assistants occurs. Typical business processes or transactions will most likely cross multiple boundaries and even countries.

What resources do corporations have today for managing information networks? They have abundant tools and systems to manage the various pieces of the networking infrastructure (see Figure 3.3). These products include reactive fault management, proactive fault management, expert systems, proxy systems, enhancements to their management platforms, and desktop management. Since these tools and systems are not integrated, some companies have taken extraordinary measures to keep their networks running smoothly, such as deploying extra technicians who specialize in certain equipment. Others install elaborate backup mechanisms to keep operations uninterrupted.

But these approaches increase the cost of managing networks. About a third of the cost is the purchase and installation of management systems; the rest is for daily operation. Most of the operational cost is salaries. Today's network management products address the management of LAN

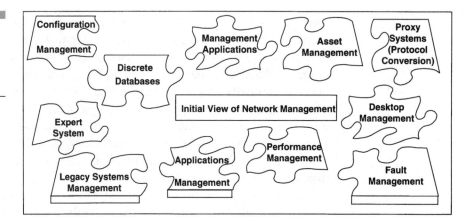

and WAN hardware components. The systems management tools, meanwhile, focus on administrative functions such as software distribution
and metering, remote backups, user administration, and operating system
interfaces.

Most major network management vendors, including those that sell
SNMP wares, promise a cohesive management infrastructure with plug-
and-play modules. Network managers, however, have found that these
products are, at best, plug and pray. To manage so many client and server
machines, automation and integration across management products and
tools must be inherent in the management infrastructure. Network and
systems management are now separate, mostly because networking
devices—such as bridges, controllers, gateways, routers, switches, and ter-
minals—have been passive rather than interactive like client and server
machines. It is imperative that corporations "systems manage" the enterprise network and not treat the networks and servers (systems) as separate
entities.

Savings Not Realized

The result of separate management operations is that corporations have
discovered that the savings and scalability that were promised by
client/server are not being realized. With the proliferation of multiple
network, systems, and applications management products, as well as help
desks and other desktop support organizations, there is an urgent need to
have an overall strategy and architecture. Command and control of the
enterprise network need not be sacrificed.

Fundamentally, protocols (such as SNMP or CMIP) and tools do not solve management problems alone. It is the processes deploying these protocols and tools that solve enterprise network problems. Networked systems management, the blurring of division between systems and network management organizations, products, technologies, and requirements suggests a "systems" thinking towards managing enterprise networks.

This paradigm should be extended to address functionality such as a common database repository, applications management, and desktop services. The best way to deliver quality service levels to end-users is to deploy an "enterprise service center" and an application suite that would automatically heal the network, fix the systems, and notify the user to what extent the service-level agreement has been met. But the products required to accomplish this goal are at least a few years away. Even if such products were available, dispatching them to manage a multiprotocol and mixed-vendor network would not be easy. A few companies are offering network and systems management frameworks and services that operate across the enterprise to provide a systemic solution to management problems.

Managing the network and systems is only getting more complicated with the advent of globalization, internets, intranets, collaborative computing, and the like. Enterprises must keep their computer and network environments flexible to allow for change, and that gets more difficult as the network grows. To further complicate matters, there is growing demand for customized management solutions using standard technology such as SNMP. This poses a greater challenge to designers and integrators to manage and keep the enterprise networks open for business.

Integrated Management Framework

What is integrated management framework? It is not a buzzword or a product. It is not a cookie-cutter approach to simple network management. It is a disciplined, enterprise-focused approach to designing, implementing, and supporting comprehensive enterprise management solutions for any kind of management requirement, and for any kind of information networked system. It addresses all aspects of the organization to be managed, all of the elements required to implement enterprise management, and all of the processes involved in designing, implementing, operating, and maintaining strategic information systems at the

Figure 3.4
Aligning Core Management Services and Systems with other IT Activities

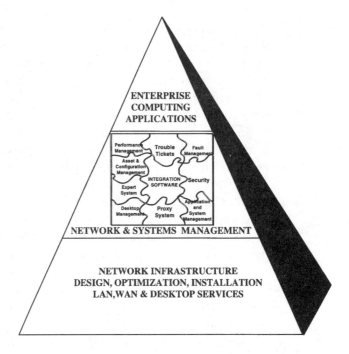

enterprise level. Figure 3.4 illustrates a properly aligned IT organization and architecture. Figure 3.5 is a logical illustration of the integrated management framework, showing how it organizes the various software ele-

Figure 3.5
Overall Architecture for Integrated Networked Systems Management

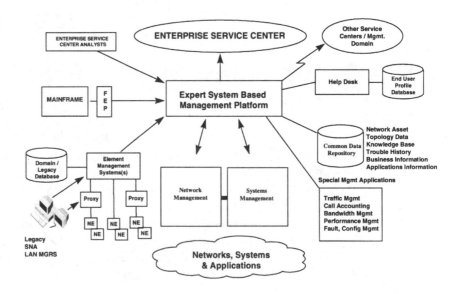

ments and processes required to implement comprehensive enterprise management, and presents them to the network operator or analyst on a single workstation or console.

Recognizing the growing scope and diversity of today's enterprise information networks, and the economic realities that prohibit their wholesale replacement, a systemic strategy for managing enterprise networks is necessary. Some of the key strategic elements are listed below.

Instrumenting the networked systems. This ensures that timely and reliable data about the systems are available to the management platform. This is a fundamental requirement for providing effective, proactive management.

Giving the element managers a key role. By integrating the element managers with the central management platform, the system can use them to monitor the network, and utilize their control capabilities. This reduces the burden both on bandwidth and on the management platform's computing cycles, while preserving the existing investment in the information networking management infrastructure.

Maintaining a central view of the information network while distributing the actual management function to the local level. This involves the use of multiple management systems and management agents, distributed locally and operating in a hierarchy, to execute management functions under the control of the central management platform. This allows centralized control while reducing the bandwidth required to perform critical management functions.

Use of automated, knowledge-based applications to increase the intelligence and level of automation available to the management system. The use of rules-based systems and expert system inference engines increases both the volume of data that can be processed and the speed at which it is processed. This enables the central management platform to prioritize data about network events based on thresholds, take actions based on operational priorities, and provide guidance based on historical data.

Applying these capabilities to the three most important aspects of end-to-end enterprise management: LANs and WANs, systems, and applications. Enterprise management only starts with networking components like LANs and WANs. It must also encompass the systems and applications that those networks support because they are the tools that accomplish crucial business functions.

This tool kit approach allows one to integrate solutions that are unique for organization, yet functional and supportable. It also allows one to develop specific management applications to expand on certain manage-

Figure 3.6
A Roadmap for
Developing an Integrated Management
Framework

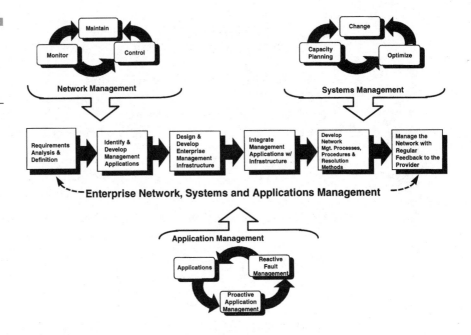

ment functions. The important thing is to recognize that no single product does it all in the world of enterprise information networking management. This is because an enterprise management system must be able to tap into the data flowing through the enterprise, understand what it is seeing in terms of management information, and exert a useful measure of control over the systems within the enterprise.

This is truly a formidable task because of the broad range of systems to be managed, and the sheer volume of objects to be managed in a typical enterprise network. Figure 3.6 is a roadmap summarizing how one could integrate various products to develop an integrated management framework implementation that brings together the diverse elements of the enterprise under unified management control. Specifically the integration process should account for the following:

- all of the systems to be managed

- the specific operational requirements imposed by
    - the nature of the organization's core business
    - the organization's internal structure
    - the geographic distribution of client functions and business units

- the specific business rules that govern how the organization conducts its core business

By consistently using this approach one could develop management interfaces to both legacy systems and proprietary systems, and to establish communications between management systems distributed across the enterprise. A key element of the integration process is the development of the necessary "glue" that binds the enterprise management systems together. Once the interfaces to the networked systems are in place and the full volume of data flowing through the enterprise is readily available, an enterprise management system must be able to perform the following four critical processes.

Filtering.   Filtering is the process by which the system identifies and selects the information from the data stream that actually impacts the operation of the enterprise (typically, this is 5 to 10 percent of all data).

Thresholding.   Thresholding is the process by which the system determines that an action should be executed based on certain conditions being met. There are two kinds of thresholds: thresholds based on minimum and maximum values (i.e., where a minimum value must be met, or a maximum value cannot be exceeded) and thresholds based on the duration and/or frequency of specific events.

Correlation.   Correlation is a crucial capability for an enterprise management system. It is the process by which the system identifies and analyzes relationships among data from multiple sources. This process can significantly reduce the number of alerts a network operator or a service center agent must respond to, and can also speed up the isolation and resolution of problems within the enterprise.

Structuring.   Structuring is the process of placing these data onscreen in a format the operator will be able to understand and respond to. It includes providing relevant background information, suggesting possible courses of action, and standardizing the data display. This is usually accomplished with a standard graphical user interface.

SUMMARY

A key benefit of the integrated management framework approach is that it allows a much more effective management paradigm for managing globally distributed information network; proactive management. This approach involves the use of modern tools and capabilities to monitor the enterprise at a level of detail and accuracy such that many problems can be identified and resolved before they impact network operations and actually impair user productivity and business functions.

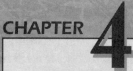

Enabling Strategies for Enterprise Management

Introduction

It is a challenging time of transition as enterprises enter the distributed computing age while globalizing their business operations and attempting to shed the centralized, tightly coupled organization and architecture of the late 1980s and early 1990s. Part of that bygone organization was the establishment of multiple, dispersed network control centers and help desks, each designed to address autonomously a different technical area within the enterprise, such as the mainframe, the LAN, the WAN, the applications, or the desktops. The problem is that in such a structure the burden of diagnosing a technical problem typically falls on the shoulders of a non-technical end-user, which eventually drains the productivity of the business. It is imperative that organizations treat information network services as service elements or products and migrate towards a vendor-of-services business model. This chapter will discuss specific enabling strategies for managing a globally distributed information network. Some key enablers are a well defined methodology, use of a real-time expert system, integrated management data repository, proactive management, desktop management, and object-oriented methodologies.

One linchpin for effective managemeant of a globally distributed (or any) information network is to design a system using an expert system and a common management information repository. These two are discussed in some detail in this chapter. Managing a distributed information network is more than just slapping together a few off-the-shelf tools. It requires a holistic architecture, skill set, and management tools and service applications. For example, managers need automated systems to report errors, manage backups, manage application performance, monitor the overall status, and manage the systems. The management of heterogeneous systems with various operating standards and systems, multivendor hardware and software systems, disparate databases, and the lack of a well-defined concept of operation has become one of the greatest concerns of large organizations that use information technology to conduct their business.

It is important that globally distributed information networks be managed by both enterprise-wide and integrated techniques. With the increasing importance of enterprise management, many vendors of LAN and WAN management systems have been expanding their management capabilities to include a wider variety of networking devices. It is important to note that such efforts are merely attempting to integrate the management functions, but are not enterprise wide. While integration may be achieved by vendors, an enterprise networking management is one that is not only integrated but also enterprise wide, crossing geographic, logical, and topological barriers to include an organization's entire networking infrastructure within an overall scheme of LANs, WANs, inter(ra)nets, desktops, systems, applications, and other telecommunications infrastructure.

Technology Trends and Analysis

As management systems vendors attempt to satisfy end-user demands and expand their solution space, the division of network management system functionality between specific element management and enterprise management is gradually blurring. While there are products that address only one of these criteria, the majority either have multiple capabilities or are blending to address the requirements of managing hybrid environments. To address the management requirements of distributed enterprise networks, therefore, involves a combination of management systems glued by an enterprise specific concept of operation methodology that spans the entire spectrum of networking management including applications and systems. Internetworking and information demands dictate seamless connections. Managing interconnecting systems is becoming critical and is an important factor in the move towards both enterprise management systems and distributed management. Distinguishing WANs and LANs is of no importance anymore as computing becomes network centric. Although many systems are claimed to be integrated, there is no real definition of the word integration and the actual levels of integration achieved vary enormously. True integration merges both physical and logical networking resource management into a single application, sharing information and correlating events across multiple elements. In addition, true integration cannot be purchased from any one vendor. Integration should and will be a custom task for an organization.

Ironically, the same market pressures that are increasing the demand for integrating network management tasks under an enterprise management system are also increasing the need to distribute the management tasks across different stations and locations. Distributed management separates management responsibilities into domains of influence instead of maintaining a strictly hierarchical management system. It is imperative that a networking management model/architecture be developed such that it is independent of any one vendor and can sustain itself regardless of the changes in the vendor offers related to management systems and applications. This dictates that an organization develop a common management information database-based management environment.

One of the most important trends seen over recent years has been the increasing lack of distinction between LANs and WANs and their internetworking with the voice networks. In an attempt to provide that network dialtone (analogous to the reliable telephone dialtone for voice communications), a wide range of networking elements and systems are being integrated using the technological advances of the intelligent hub. With the computing cost and transmission bandwidth cost rapidly decreasing, network designs and architectures are flattening and shifting from hierarchical to distributed peer-to-peer configurations. Irrespective of the networking environment, it is a business imperative that organizations manage their network dialtone and the information that rides on that dialtone. As previously discussed, organizations are globalizing their operations, and a distributed networking management environment that supports such an operation is of paramount importance. Distributed management involves separating management responsibilities into domains of influence instead of maintaining a strictly hierarchical management system. A distributed management environment enables an organization to access, control, and manage any of their networking resources irrespective of the operator's location.

Integrated Management

Integrated management of information networks is a business imperative and organizations have no choice if they want to survive the rising cost of managing networks and systems in pieces. Functional integration is emerging as a major area of endeavor, where information from different types of elements and management domains can be coordinated and acted upon in a meaningful fashion. For example, help desk and networking management can both be effected through a common data repository where the end-user information and the network environment information are normalized, consolidated, integrated, and stored. Likewise, such an integrated application can be used for the resolution of multiple alarms reported by different devices generated by one fault. Rather than the operator having to find which of several dozens of alarms actually relates to the true fault by manually resolving the alarms generated by subsidiary devices (e.g. hubs, routers) the expert system could isolate and resolve the problem.

Real-Time Expert System

An expert system is problem-solving software that embodies specialized knowledge in a narrow task domain to do work usually performed by trained and skilled humans. In effect, it solves the problems using a computer model of expert human reasoning, reaching the same conclusions that the human expert would reach if faced with a comparable problem.

Expert systems should be thought of as computer systems that attempt to perform similar tasks as knowledge systems. But for an expert system the knowledge usually has been extracted directly from an expert and deliberately represented "as it is." Thus, in an expert system the knowledge has not been analyzed, modeled, and normalized.

The motivation for developing an "intelligent" management system for managing enterprise networks is the dissemination of rare and costly expertise, and more efficient use of the human expert, decreased cost of operations, higher systems availability, and early fault detection, isolation, and resolution. Above all, the most important reason is the formalization and clarification of knowledge that results from having human experts make their reasoning explicit. For discussion purposes the expert system, management platform, and proxy agents, products offered by Gensym Corporation, Hewlett-Packard, and Bridgeway Corporation respectively, are referenced throughout this book.

Real-Time Expert Management Systems

Traditional approaches to network management are not coping with evolving requirements and technological advances and will work even less in the future. The complexity and diversity of the management problems facing distributed applications over a globally distributed network is enormous. Integrated management of such networks consists of many real-time decisions being made upon a large body of constantly shifting data. These continual variations often lead to labor-intensive applications that are prime candidates for automation. In addition, an object-oriented design of expert management systems allows for the realization of large management applications.

Real time means many things to many people. It should be noted that real time does not mean fast response only. Real-time expert systems must also respond predictably within a given time interval, reason under pressure, and adjust the focus of their attention to cope with upcoming hard or soft real-time deadlines. Current expert systems still have a way to go before they can fully satisfy all of these concerns. With the available technology, implementing real-time expert management systems for managing a globally distributed networked system environment requires an interesting mix of products and services.

The real-time expert management system allows the representation of deep and complex knowledge about the network, both analytic and heuristic. Graphic and structured natural language interfaces allow the user to construct knowledge bases for dynamic network service applications, to test expert system behavior under dynamic conditions, and to validate knowledge bases under various dynamic scenarios. For an expert management system intended to operate in real time, several characteristics of dynamic domains of the distributed services network impose requirements on the knowledge representation and should be carefully planned and implemented.

As the issues of time relationships and dynamic behavior become important, it is imperative to depart from static management systems and move towards real-time expert management systems. These systems will be capable of applying thousands of rule frames of knowledge, and of performance in real time for widely distributed and complex distributed networked systems environment operations.

Real-Time Fault Diagnosis

One of the significant problems (or a challenge) in managing a globally distributed network is real-time fault diagnosis. The objective of fault diagnosis is to pinpoint and correct problems that occur in dynamic systems. However, the objective of real-time fault diagnosis is to perform these tasks within a timeframe that allows continued, safe operation of the system and before the end-users of the network notice the problem. The timeframe for real-time diagnosis can vary dramatically depending on the system being diagnosed. For mission-critical networked applications, these timeframes have to be carefully characterized with a good balance between reliable delivery of services and reliable operation of the network.

Expert system-based management systems are capable of continuously monitoring more variables with greater accuracy and faster response time than human beings. To fully realize the advantages, however, an expert diagnosis system must be able to access real-time management information, intelligently interpret that management information, communicate with decision-making entities, and initiate corrective actions if necessary. To accomplish this type of real-time fault diagnosis requires integration of existing network management technologies and advanced software systems.

Specification of a Real-Time Diagnosis Environment

Before a diagnosis system can intelligently interpret data, knowledge must be added to the system by a human expert. This knowledge can include models of system behavior and interactions, and human experience and interpretations. Collectively, this knowledge is referred to as a knowledge base (KB). Knowledge-based diagnosis systems can achieve greater sophistication, sensitivity, and flexibility than can be achieved with fault-tolerant hardware or simple alarming systems alone. Hence, an important requirement for realizing a real-time fault diagnosis system is developing a good knowledge base.

Probably the most difficult task in developing a real-time expert management system is creation of the KB; therefore, a software environment for real-time diagnosis must have a user interface tailored for the knowledge-base developer. Due to the dynamic nature and complexities of the distributed networks and systems, the knowledge-base developer's interface should support rapid, incremental development, so the developer can quickly build, test, and modify diagnosis strategies. The developer's interface should represent knowledge in a way that is logical and understandable and should closely match the domain expert's mental models so that other domain experts can immediately comprehend the KB. Lastly, the developer's interface should be sufficiently intuitive and robust to allow the domain expert to construct the KB without the aid of a knowledge engineer. Knowledge acquisition and translation are inherent bottlenecks in the construction of a KB.

A complete environment for real-time fault diagnosis should be capable of performing the following functions:

- filtering and statistically analyzing noisy data
- detecting fault symptoms (proactive management)
- identifying root causes
- generating, filtering, and managing alarms
- providing advice and reasoning
- recognizing recurring problems
- determining appropriate corrective actions

To communicate with network operators and managers, the expert management environment should have a different user interface tailored to operations personnel. The network operator's interface should concentrate on display of information and provide facilities to quickly browse the KB so that the basis for diagnostic conclusions can be understood. Information filtering and prioritization are crucial to avoid overloading and distracting the human decision maker at the network management center. The system should allow human confirmation or override of conclusions and actions, and the interface should support creation of a log containing all system conclusions, explanations, and advice, and all user comments and inputs.

Advances in object-oriented expert systems have allowed new methodologies to be used in the construction of large-scale management systems. Among the new aspects are knowledge representations that allow graphical construction that are understood by an expert system, and that automatically become a deep knowledge representation of the structure of interactions of objects. The object-oriented representation allows definition of problem behavior to be expressed generically, applying to whole classes of objects, and the understanding of interaction structure by the expert system then allows diagnosis to proceed from the object instance for which the problem behavior is detected, looking upstream for problem sources or downstream for effects. This design approach significantly simplifies the complex correlation of alarms and events required to manage a distributed network.

The combination of methodologies discussed above, together with advances in reasoning paradigms, will together allow us to realize a complex real-time intelligent networking management system.

Object-Oriented Development Methodology

The computer industry in general, and networking management in particular, are rapidly moving to object-oriented technology. Specifically, object-oriented databases are becoming the standard management information repositories, and object-oriented programming techniques are used to produce many of the new management service applications. The end result for users should be more powerful and stable management systems. Several vendors have evolved their products' repositories from flat files to relational databases and finally to object-oriented databases. A management infrastructure with object and event services is imperative in the development of a management environment that is capable of managing a globally distributed information network.

The advancements in graphical user interfaces and workstation technologies has reduced the resources and time required to implement graphical domain definition. In distributed networks, messages, service type, and delivery portals form an interactive network. By representing these as objects, in the object-oriented programming sense, and by letting the graphical connectivity or relationships define the possible interactions, a significant part of the domain definition is done graphically. The cloning and connecting of objects defines the interaction and message handling and transport part of the network. This is both faster than conventional programming and easier to modify and understand.

An object is a convenient item to represent structure, graphic image, and other characteristics. One may wish to change the object class, adding attributes or behaviors, for example. This may be desired even for a domain that is populated with objects already. Thus the methodology to allow editing of object classes, defining new attributes, changing existing attributes, and modifying behavior is all built into the software. An object class can be changed, and the already existing instances will be changed in conformity with this.

To simplify the creation and manipulation of objects, and the definition of rules and other forms of knowledge, a structured fourth-generation language or natural language would be beneficial. As objects are cloned and connected, an interactive network of dynamic objects is created, and the expert system can use this for its reasoning. The interacting network of dynamic objects (message header, service type, and delivery mechanism) represents the deep knowledge of the domain. This is typically the knowledge possessed by the designers of the enterprise application itself. If an object-oriented KB were developed using the above methodology, the designer's knowledge could be augmented with the knowledge possessed by network operators or others with experience in operating and/or supporting the network. Such knowledge may be expressed as rules, which may refer to behavior over time. Rules and other forms of knowledge are typically expressed in general terms. This allows knowledge to look for types of behavior and provides economy of representation, which is easier to implement and maintain.

Another design concept is the propagation of reasoning via connected objects. Reasoning about connected objects allows the expert system to look for causes of problems, and to start looking for effects earlier (proactive management), before established thresholds are reached or violated.

Hence the integration of object-oriented design, advanced graphics, generic characterization of object behavior, and using connectivity of objects is an effective way of putting intelligence into managing a widely distributed network environment. A basic functional depiction of a real-time expert system is shown in Figure 4.1.

Management Information Model of the Network

To sufficiently characterize different properties of an information network, it is essential to outline an integrated information model of the network. The model consists of managed objects, the relationship between the managed objects, and attributes associated with the managed object. This section describes the main elements of the model and their role and importance within the model.

This model provides information for proactive and reactive management for real-time and intelligent operation of a distributed services net

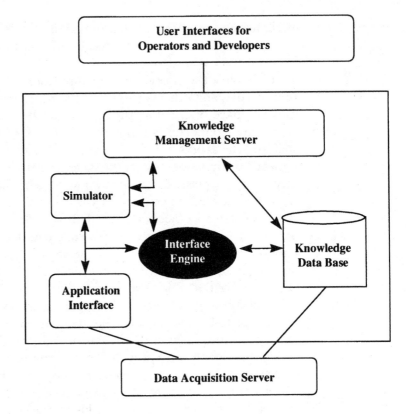

work. The information includes monitoring, control, diagnosis, optimization of network performance, and automatic corrective action. The model is primarily problem-management focused, although it provides additional information necessary for other aspects of networking management. As discussed before, one of the significant challenges for a distributed network is accurate isolation (to correlate different events and alarms) of problems in the network in a timely manner. In order to be able to correlate events in a heterogeneous network, the networking management system must access management information about the network. In actual networks, this information is contained in highly varying formats and is distributed among several elements in the network.

Managed Objects.   Managed objects are network elements, such as processors, switches, links, and other service and business applications in the network. The management information model consists of three types of managed objects: physical, logical, and functional.

Physical objects characterize the physical network components like switches, modems, processors, facilities, etc. They are used to physically locate a network element that should be controlled or is in a nonnormal state. Logical objects represent logical properties of the network elements. They are used to provide the appropriate user interface to the operators of the network (e.g., network connectivity map). The functional objects represent the functionality of the network elements or the different services and building blocks of the enterprise network. Functional objects are used to monitor the behavior of the network in real-time conditions, to detect exception events in the network or potential problems that could lead to unreliable performance of the network.

Relationships Between Managed Objects.   Relationships between managed objects support management of the network activities. For our discussion, we can distinguish the following three types of relationships: physical containment and its implementation, logical containment and its implementation, and functional containment.

Physical containment is a hierarchical relation between physical objects in which one of the objects contains the others. For example, an EDI service of an electronic commerce network contains a message header validation subsystem, an input subsystem, a message handling subsystem, and a delivery subsystem. Physical objects and associated physical containment relationships form a hierarchical tree called a physical management information tree. The containment relationships are formed to the lowest level of the component that one wishes to control and monitor. In the above example, the lowest level of the tree would be the delivery subsystem, as this is the last event before a transaction leaves the network.

Logical containment is a hierarchical relation between logical objects in which one of the objects contains the others. For example, an EDI service logically contains a user agent subsystem, a message handling subsystem, a message transport subsystem, and a delivery subsystem. These subsystems represent logical objects and each has its own logical constituents. Logical objects and associated logical containment relationships form a hierarchical tree called a logical management information tree.

Functional containment, like physical and logical containment, is a hierarchical relation between functional objects in which one object consists of the others. For example, the overall network services complex is a functional object that represents all functions of the network. The overall network switching complex functionally contains message input, a message handler, a message transporter, message delivery gateways, and types of network services as subordinate functional objects. Each of these subordinate functional objects has its own subordinates.

Functional objects and associated functional containment relationships form a hierarchical tree called a functional management information tree.

Physical implementation is a relationship between physical and logical objects. It represents a mapping between the logical properties incorporated within a logical object into the corresponding physical network equipment. Logical implementation is a relation between logical and functional objects. It represents a mapping between the functionality of a functional object into the corresponding manageable logical object. Logical implementations are extremely useful in the analysis and correlation of alarms. When an alarm denotes the faulty logical object, the logical object can easily be mapped into the corresponding functional object via logical implementation relation. The thus obtained functional object shows which network functionality is deteriorating and how the network is performing. For example, message handling is a functional object that is logically implemented within a processor.

Attributes of the Managed Objects.   Attributes represent additional information on the static and dynamic properties of the managed objects. Static properties are characteristics of the objects that do not change in a long time period. For example, the location of a transaction servicing queue as implemented (or designed) is static barring any changes to the actual design or architecture of the networked system. Dynamic properties are characteristics of the objects that are subject to relatively frequent changes in time. For example, the message queue size for a particular network service type is dynamic and is subject to frequent changes during normal operation of the network. Each managed object has its own set of attributes. Some of the attributes that are of interest for distributed networks are the following:

- managed object identification
- location of the managed object
- type of the managed object (physical, logical, functional)
- status of the managed object
- relationship to other managed objects
- list of possible alarms related to the managed objects
- corrective actions for fault resolution of the managed object

Managed objects and their associated attributes could be implemented using a fourth-generation (or natural) structured language graphical user interface, as discussed earlier in this chapter. The model discussed thus far defined the managed objects, as applicable to a distributed networked system environment, their relations, and their attributes. The managed objects could be hierarchically organized, enabling one to manage a network either globally distributed or centralized. The information model should be implemented into a knowledge database. The elements of the database will be records that represent managed objects of the network. The management information model itself is suitable for the various network management applications.

Common Management Information Repository

A common management information repository (CMIR) is a major integration component of the integrated management framework as discussed in the previous chapter. It should be designed as a database application with the appropriate systems and user interfaces. The CMIR discussed in this book was developed while the author was at I-NET Corporation, now a Wang company. Figure 4.2 illustrates a representation of the CMIR components. Some of the key requirements and functions that should be performed by the CMIR are as follows:

- Serve as a data integration platform between different management systems, providing exchange and consistency of data in the proprietary databases supported by the other systems and a central storage of static and dynamic data related to all types of managed objects.

- Provide a cross-platform user access to the data generated by different management systems, with convenient and flexible graphical user interface, intended for operators, systems administrators, and analysts working on a variety of operating system environments.

- Provide a system interface between the database management system carrying the management data and the other management services delivery tools, including the expert system, end-user support systems, performance measurement systems, etc.

- Enable a standard method to access the management data from any custom application so that these systems can use and maintain data stored in the CMIR database, as well as enable one to design an effective decision support system.

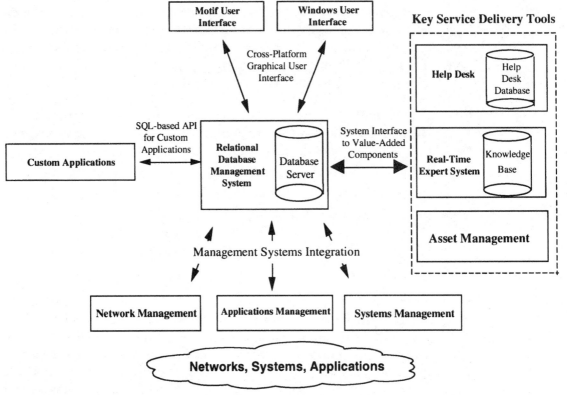

Figure 4.2   Common Management Information Repository
Components and Interfaces

CMIR as a Data Integration Platform

Being a management data integration platform, the CMIR should support the data exchange between the management systems incorporated in an integrated management framework environment. In this role, the common management information repository should perform the following functions:

1. Provide exchange and consistency of the data in the proprietary databases supported by the relevant management systems. The constituents of an integrated management framework environment could be:

   - network management platforms and systems
   - systems and applications management tools
   - configuration management systems
   - end-user and help desk tools

2. Serve as a central storage of static and dynamic data containing information about all types of managed objects, including:

   - networks, communications hardware and software
   - desktop/workstations hardware and software
   - system objects, such as all types of servers, databases, and utilities

Static data, such as IP addresses, workstation types, names, etc., are updated in sync with the relatively rare and slow changes of system configuration, whereas dynamic data, such as network events, performance data, trouble tickets, etc., are stored in historical time-stamped records.

CMIR as a Cross-Platform Access Tool

Since the CMIR data are stored in the relational database, it is natural to provide the users with the capability to search, extract, and possibly update this information whenever there is a need to analyze or modify the status of the managed systems and applications. CMIR should be designed as a client/server database application with the following functions:

1. Provide effective and user-friendly graphical user interface for operators, system administrators, analysts, and business managers to access the systems management data from the client workstations. This allows the systems management functions to be distributed among several points of control with the appropriate access authorization.

2. Give users the capability for presenting the architecture of the entire management system, or any detailed information on a selected subsystem, segment, network element, or other components; this representation can be done independently of the status and accessibility of the management systems that delivered the corresponding data.

3. Perform conversion and consolidation of the historical data reflecting the dynamics of the managed objects and make an appropriate analysis of these data. Information-rich reporting capabilities of the client/server applications could be used for generating statistical and analytical reports that may be needed for systems optimization and enhancement. This function is analogous to a data warehouse of the information networking environment, enabling decision makers with the appropriate support systems and statistics.

CMIR as a System Interface for Other Management Systems

The relational database management system, which is a core of the CMIR, should be associated with a standard applications programming interface. This capability will supply systems designers with a convenient method of interfacing the CMIR with other management systems and applications. Typical components of an enterprise management system include the following:

- Real-time expert system comprising the knowledge base and inference engine that performs filtering and correlation of events, alarms, and other functions related to the networking environment.

- Help-desk applications that need access to the CMIR for obtaining appropriate information related to trouble ticketing and sending back consolidated information on the results of trouble resolution.

- Asset and configuration management systems that require consistency of management data to provide effective integrated solutions.

Of particular importance is the symbiosis of the database management system and real-time expert system. The expert system has its own knowledge base with the object-oriented model of the managed environment, and also the rules, relations, and procedures needed for intelligent processing of the states and events in this environment. But, in order to run the process, it requires that the actual data to be obtained. For this purpose it uses the CMIR as a data server. On the other hand, the CMIR obtains from the expert system additional information, resulting from the inference processing, filtering, and correlation, and this information is delivered to the end-user through the unified graphical user interface, on a multitude of operating system platforms.

CMIR as Database Interface for Management Applications

Custom management applications can perform special processing of management information such as generating graphical representation of systems and network architecture (network maps), changing configuration of certain managed objects, etc.

The CMIR, if implemented, will provide an ideal medium for bringing together information related to network, systems, and applications management. It allows for correlation of managed objects and events in

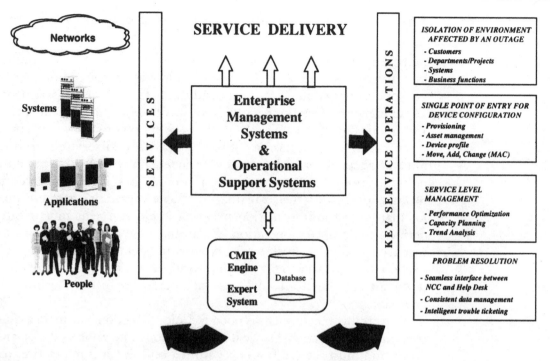

Figure 4.3 Benefits of Common Management Information Repository

multiple environments, especially with the help of the enabling expert system.

Being a core component of an integrated management framework environment, the CMIR will significantly enhance the services delivered by a variety of management and decision support systems that could be considered partners in the framework of integrated management solution. In summary, the CMIR provides the following additional functions:

- presentation and update of information networking environment configuration

- monitoring of network events

- monitoring of systems and specific applications performance events

- consolidation and synchronization of asset data base

- enabling billing and chargeback systems

- enhancing end-user support systems

The benefits of a common management information repository application is described in Figure 4.3.

Defining a Concept of Operation

Managing a widely distributed information network is becoming increasingly complex. As the business world realizes the importance of network-centric computing, it demands more from the IT departments. These higher expectations result from increased business competition and improvements in IT, causing the work process to evolve for entire organizations and increasing network dependence. IT service personnel must be adept at managing not only the technology, but also the business operations, vendors, customers, and more importantly include the business process of their organizations. The organization responsible for managing the information networking environment must clearly define its concept of operation, explaining how the network will be managed vis-à-vis its business functions and operations. For example, it may not be necessary to tag a high priority action for an isolated failure if the affected environment does not interfere with normal business operation.

Networking management is not a technical function, but more a complex business operation. Hence it has to demonstrate value to the organization and must act as a business within a business. It is imperative that the networking management personnel posses many skills directly related to networking technology, including financial planning, marketing, negotiating, benchmarking, etc. Managing information networks is both strategic and tactical. Organizations must emphasize its importance to the business and treat it as a means to an end with costs that must be managed. The realm of networking management generally focuses on managing the technology and, more specifically, managing networking problems. Networking management systems tend to focus narrowly on a set of related functions regarding how the technology is working or being accounted for.

Managing the information networking environment involves not only managing the underlying technology but also managing the services that the technology provides. The end-users are not concerned about some inoperative networking element, but they are concerned when their business function is unavailable due to disruption in a specific service of the networking environment. Information networking management must provide the capabilities to manage the infrastructure and meet their customer service requirements cost effectively. The information networking services management environment (INSME) should also enhance the overall effectiveness of all the stakeholders by supporting tactical and long-range planning based on in-depth analysis of performance data collected from daily operations. Both daily and long-term INSME functions are needed to meet the following objectives:

- ensure the efficient use of networking infrastructure systems and personnel resources
- enhance service delivery by initiating end-to-end service management
- accommodate end-user and customer preferences
- initiate performance-based management to improve processes
- collect and distribute infrastructure and service performance information
- support strategy generation, evaluation, and feedback

It is essential that, during its life cycle, the INSME provide automation for predicting when and where networking infrastructure may be affected by failures or degradation. The INSME should support the customers with accurate, timely information about system conditions, available alternatives, expected delays for restoral of service, and other constraints. This information will enable the users of the information network to more effectively plan and carry out their business functions. The concept of operation for managing the networking environment should provide the means for management of information so that relevant, sufficient, accurate, and timely information can be delivered upon request to the users who are connected to the network. The management information infrastructure should have an operational impact on end-to-end services and performance of other systems that require data or information for operation.

Client/Server Drives Management Paradigm Shift

Convergence of network and systems management should occur not at the technology domain, but rather at the functional domain via discipline-specific applications that rely on both platform services and intelligent agents. Most organizations have some sort of event management systems in the network domain currently managing their IT infrastructure. As client/server applications are being developed and deployed, users are finding it necessary to monitor the systems and applications that their businesses rely on. Figure 4.4 summarizes some critical technical and functional components of an integrated enterprise management platform to manage a distributed information network.

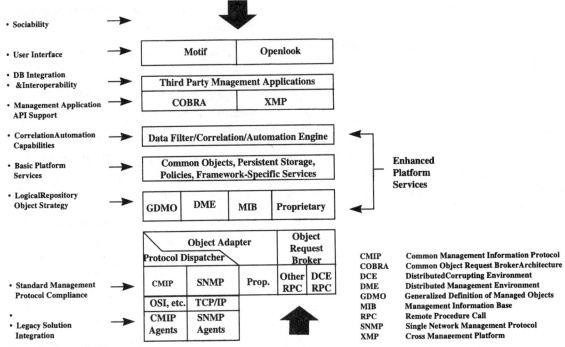

Figure 4.4   NSM Technical and Functional Requirements

A complete systems event management offering consists of six components: agents, midlevel managers, event storage, state managers, console applications, and administration/configuration utilities. Many of these components map closely to those of a distributed performance management system.

Agents.   Whereas mainframes had console messages, distributed systems have events. The efficient detection and routing of a noteworthy event in a complex system is difficult because of the volume of activity in a typical server, and the number of possible (and interacting) things that can constitute an event. The processor-intensive task of detecting an event from raw data is shared between the agent and the midlevel manager. Simple events (a single trigger or a small number of local events) are determined at the agent. Systems for which no agent is available can feed messages to the midlevel management layer event detection. Increased agent intelligence can reduce event traffic volume and improve response time at the expense of processor overhead at every monitored node. Finding an ideal balance between agent and midlevel manager processing is a long-term objective. Configuring the agents for each node and defining the event conditions constitute a significant project. Many implementations of event management products take longer and some get abandoned. Organizations must pay close attention to this important phase of the project as it is crucial to providing the management services at the least cost possible.

The Middle Tier. A central console cannot be used to directly manage more than a few dozen nodes if any significant processing is being done. Rather than proliferate management consoles, most vendors are moving to deliver midlevel managers (domain management systems) that enable nodes to be segmented into domains. By offloading the agent, the console, and the WAN through local processing and consolidation, the domain manager is key to a scalable networking management infrastructure. Processed events are sent from the domain managers to the state manager. This component keeps track of the status of each of the monitored resources and its agents.

Console Applications. Current console applications for event management systems provide little more than color-coded maps and message response scripting. True event/console automation will be critical to managing a distributed client/server environment. The event management systems, as currently evolving, will supply the requisite infrastructure to support automation.

Enterprise Networking Services Management

The benefits of integrating element management systems are significant and generate enormous cost savings for operating the network. However, an integrated networking management system (INMS) is not trivial, and involves careful planning and adhering to a consistent architecture and management paradigm. This section describes some evolutionary approaches to integrating such systems and the various challenges involved in doing so. Integrating different element management systems also provides an opportunity to distribute some of the management applications and functions across the various management systems. This is a key and rapidly growing functionality for managing distributed applications like enterprise services, which are usually globally distributed with differing time zones and temporal requirements.

One of the important reasons for integrating different element management systems is to provide the tools to coordinate the management of a large distributed enterprise services network consisting of multivendor products and services from end to end. This underscores the need for sophisticated but user-friendly interfaces that would ideally present multiple management and support systems in a uniform and consistent method. The motivation behind integration is to collect all status reports and alarm signals, no matter what brand of equipment they come from, and present network operators with only the most useful and urgent information. Such an effort might involve providing color-coded overview maps of the network, but also would let operators zoom in on small details anywhere they wish. Expert systems software or other rule-based software systems might filter incoming events and alarms, give detailed advice, and even act automatically to, say, reroute traffic around a failed component. The next sections will discuss some requirements for the integrated management of distributed networked systems environment and describe an evolutionary architecture and design for such a system.

System Requirements

The integrated management of a distributed network requires careful planning of a system that not only meets the current requirements but also provides for growth and for managing additional and evolving network services and networking architectures. This system should be architected and designed as a platform for the rapid deployment of networking management applications and services. It must therefore be extensible in areas including platform and infrastructure, standards conformance, expert system requirements, and integrated databases.

Platform and Infrastructure.　The platform and infrastructure includes areas like graphical user interface, interface to element management systems, and integrated relational database. Some of the high-level requirements include the following:

Graphical User Interface.

■ *Map Applications.* As new networks and services become available to the enterprise services network, management applications will be added to the management platform. Applications must be easily integrated to the map interface to preserve the common management methods of the management system.

■ *Map Symbols.* New or existing map applications may require symbols to be added to the user interface. The type or number of symbols in a map must not be limited by anything other than system resources.

Interface to Element Management Systems. When the integrated management system is initially deployed, it supports certain communication methods. However, this system should support extensions to the following:

■ *Managed Object Definitions.* The integrated management system must allow for the incremental addition to its set of managed objects definitions. It must support the addition of MIBs as new or enhanced devices are added to the network services environment.

■ *Management Protocols.* As network devices provide support for emerging management protocols, the integrated management platform should support applications developed to communicate with them.

Integrated Relational Database. The foundation for a comprehensive management of a networked systems environment is the ability to document and manage all of the devices and equipment and their connectivity within the network. A physical and configuration management application requires a relational database that is well integrated into the overall management platform. This configuration management application provides detailed information about the entire networking infrastructure, including the real-world location of network devices, their technical characteristics, and their physical connectivity. Some examples of data stored in the relational database are:

■ network statistics
■ event filters
■ managed network topology
■ expert system KB
■ application integration (help desk, asset management, etc.)

Standards Conformance. The integrated management platform will rely on its conformance to standards to maximize its compatibility with new and existing off-the-shelf management applications and provide a foundation for rapid custom networking management application development. These standards include:

■ graphical user interface—X.11/Motif, OSF/DME, etc.
■ management communication—OSF/DME, XOM/XMP API access to SNMP, CMIP, and CMOT protocols

- database management system—SQL (ANSI standard, etc.) or OSQL (object-oriented structured query language) for an object-oriented database management system

Expert System Requirements.   The scope of the requirements and discussion on expert-system module of the integrated management platform (or system) is limited to problem detection, isolation, and resolution applications. However, the expert system design and architecture will accommodate other management service applications.

The objective of fault management is to isolate and correct problems that occur in a dynamic environment. These tasks have to be performed within a timeframe that allows continued, correct operation of the enterprise services network. Economic incentives for real-time fault management include service quality, customer satisfaction, and timely problem resolution. The expert system should have the following basic capabilities to provide the operators with any real-time benefits:

- access real-time data
- intelligently interpret data
- communicate with operators, when necessary
- log all activities
- recognize recurring problems
- correlate multiple alarms for a common problem
- initiate corrective actions
- automatically generate trouble tickets
- automatically route for new facilities

In order to improve operator productivity, a key function of network management is to correlate multiple events and/or alarms, filter out sympathy alarms, and inform the operator of the most probable cause of the problem. Once this task has been accomplished, the next step is to automate that resolution or provide the operator with an option for human intervention or other features, such as trouble report generation, etc.

Management Platform Architecture

The most important architectural strategy is simply to have a comprehensive architecture for managing enterprise networks. The problem would be utterly intractable without an architectural framework for such a complex network. The architecture is described in terms of the integrated management platform software architecture. The platform provides the infrastructure to support a set of enterprise network management service applications. Platform technology is evolving, but the real solutions for managing an enterprise network are found in the management applications, the critical ingredient for implementing the solutions demanded by a globally distributed enterprise network. Integrated management applications that share information and activate each other increase operator productivity and leverage the investment in platforms and management service applications.

The management platform architecture is comprised of three primary components: the element management system protocol converter engine, the management server, and an expert system server. However, the most important components of the integrated management platform are the management applications. The integrated management platform architecture describes three examples: commercial off-the-shelf (COTS) management applications, custom management applications developed specifically to address an enterprise services network, and utility applications like an expert system and physical network management application.

There are several aspects to management application integration: the vertical integration to the platform and the horizontal integration among the various management service applications. Quality management applications must be closely integrated with the platform so they can take advantage of common services and operate efficiently. Management applications must be integrated with each other so that information can flow between them to carry out management tasks. The three primary components—protocol converter engine, management server, and expert system engine—are described below. The complexities and challenges involved in multilevel management application integration will become obvious as we progress through the design of the integrated management system.

Protocol Converter Engine.   Currently, the predominant management information communication protocol is the SNMP; it is rapidly gaining popularity and acceptance in the network management industry. The CMIP is the OSI communication protocol for network management. It offers an increased level of functionality when compared to the SNMP. However, implementing the CMIP places greater resource demands on both the network managers and the managed network elements. Subsequently, its acceptance and application by vendors and applications software providers is limited and slow. The integrated management system that is discussed here will be based on the SNMP as its means of communication between the management server and all managed network elements. Support and change to the CMIP, as applications and network elements become more available, will be a minor effort.

Network Event Process. In the platform architecture, all asynchronous events (e.g., alarms) are conveyed to the management server via the *trap* message of the SNMP management protocol. Network devices (and element managers) that do not support the SNMP directly must rely on a protocol converter to translate their native protocol to SNMP. This protocol converter is commonly termed a *proxy*. A typical integrated management event process is shown in Figure 4.5. Devices should be interfaced directly to the system running the SNMP proxy agent. In general, asynchronous ports and protocols could be used to communicate with these devices. The proxy agent will act as a gateway, transforming messages received from the device into SNMP traps. The proxy agent will incorporate tunable parameters for filtering and forwarding messages.

Management Process. In the management platform architecture, a management request and the ensuing response from a managed device will

Figure 4.5 Typical Integrated Management and Event Process

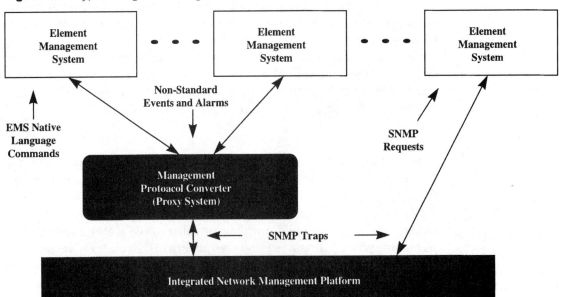

be conveyed using the SNMP requests: SNMP Set and SNMP Get. As in the case of the event process, non-SNMP devices could rely on a proxy to translate the requests into a form that it supports. For many of the managed devices in a typical network this translation consists of receiving the SNMP request and mapping that into an appropriate console dialogue in order to query or control some target managed system parameter, the result of which will again be translated as the response to the SNMP requests and conveyed back to the manager.

SNMP Proxy. There are several off-the-shelf network management tools that allows users to build applications to exchange network management data with a number of industry-standard network managers. These tools allow users to quickly build management applications without using a programming language. One such tool is an SNMP proxy software system. The primary purpose of this system is to convert non-SNMP devices into an SNMP device, along with provision for developing custom MIBs. For the purposes of describing the integrated management of enterprise networks, we will be using a proxy system for interfacing with proprietary devices, where necessary.

SNMP Proxy Components. The structure of an SNMP proxy is usually based on two interdependent concepts: its architecture and its objects. The proxy's world consists of three fundamental, user-defined object types—events, actions, and rules—that enable the user to determine what inputs the proxy will recognize and how it will respond.

Proxy Interface Modules. The interface modules usually provide an API to a specific set of formats and protocols enabling the exchange of data with the element management systems on one end and the integrated management system on the other end. Most proxy applications will use one or more of these interface modules to exchange data with other systems. The two pertinent interface modules are the Async/ASCII and the SNMP modules.

In the Async/ASCII interface module, user applications can request data from a given port or multiple ports or send data out to a device via another asynchronous port. One can specify the asynchronous communications port parameters and type of connection desired. Using these tools, one can effectively develop an SNMP proxy agent for non-SNMP managed elements.

The proxy system can be used to write applications to act both as SNMP managers and agents. Agent services include the ability to construct custom proxy agents for non-SNMP devices and the ability to support the SNMP multiplexing (SMUX) protocol. The SMUX protocol allows proxy agents to reside on the same host as existing SNMP agents. Some of these proxy systems also come with a MIB-builder that could be used in conjunction with the SNMP interface module. This tool allows a user to construct ASN.1-compliant MIBs by specifying the objects that are to be placed in the enterprise-specific MIB and their object identifiers. This shields the developer from detailed ASN.1 syntax and rules.

Types of Events and Actions.   The process of identifying meaningful enterprise network events and actions is a significant part of managing such a network. The proxy systems usually provide facilities to aid the user in this process by allowing a user to specify the following events and actions:

System Events.   System events are descriptions of the status of executing programs: termination of a named program and the receipt of output from a named program.

Miscellaneous Events.   Miscellaneous events are the expiration of timers or the occurrence of pseudo-events; both timers and pseudo-events are user defined.

Timer Events.   Proxy systems have the capability of detecting the expiration of user-defined timers.

Pseudo-events.   Pseudo-events are used to record the occurrence of event sequences and support limited procedural control over proxy rules. This is an excellent feature in hierarchical problem management and multi-paradigm knowledge representation. For example, suppose one has defined three events, EventA, EventB, and EventC. One may wish to have an action taken whenever EventC occurs, following the first occurrence of EventA and EventB. One would set a pseudo-event to record the occurrence of EventA and EventB and then take the action when the pseudo-event and EventC occur. Pseudo-events are events that can be generated directly from the action list within a rule.

Asynchronous Communications Events (Async Events).   Async communications events describe text messages that have been received on the asynchronous interface module. Many WAN devices, such as modems and switches, use asynchronous communications to send messages to controlling systems.

SNMP Events. SNMP events are descriptions of messages that are received via the SNMP interface module.

Systems Actions. Systems actions are descriptions of requests to execute a program or for writing messages to a file.

Miscellaneous Actions. Miscellaneous actions set the expiration time for timers and declare the occurrence of pseudo-events.

Async Communications Actions. Async communications actions describe text messages to be sent to devices. These are done via the asynchronous interface module.

SNMP Actions. SNMP actions are descriptions of requests and messages that are sent to other devices that support the SNMP protocol. The SNMP interface module is used to send the requests and messages. Proxy systems support three types of SNMP requests: Get, GetNext, and Set. In addition to these requests, the SNMP interface may be used to send unsolicited messages or traps to devices that support the SNMP protocol.

Management Platform Server. The integrated management's central component is the enterprise network management server as depicted in Figure 4.6. It serves as the central communication mechanism for all network management applications and also functions as a graphical user interface server for the operators.

As a communications infrastructure, its role is defined in two modes of operation. First, it provides the means to propagate asynchronous network events to specific management applications that need to receive them in order to perform their intended functions. Second, it allows management applications to initiate requests on network elements or their element management systems in order to provide monitor and control capability. These two modes are described as two separate processes: the enterprise network event process, and the enterprise network management process.

Enterprise Network Event Process. In the network event process, the network management server is tasked with receiving incoming network events and passing them along to management applications that have requested such notifications. These events may originate from network elements or their element management systems (external to the management server), or from management applications in order to communicate with other management applications running on the platform/server. For example, in the first case an element management system (or proxy sys-

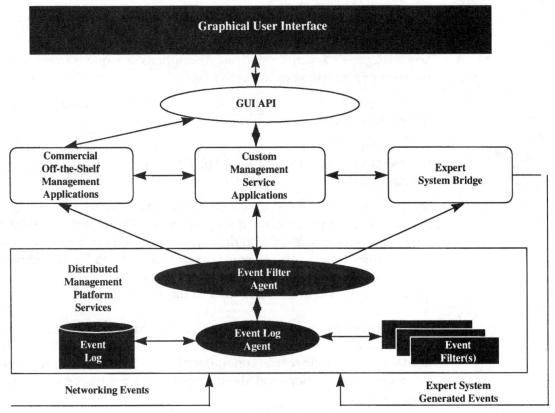

Figure 4.6 Components of Integrated Management Platform for Messaging Networks

tem) creates an event to notify all concerned that it has detected a fault condition. In the second case the expect system has evaluated this notification (along with other conditions) and has determined that the network map display window should be updated to reflect a root cause condition. It creates its own event, and all applications that have registered prior to its creation are notified.

Management Platform and Events.   Several components of the integrated management platform are involved in the process of handling enterprise network events.

Management Platform Infrastructure.   The management infrastructure provides a common foundation for communication and integration between all services available to network and systems management applications developed for management integration. The purpose of the management infrastructure is to simplify the problems of network and systems management by providing a single interface between management applications (expert system bridge), agents (element managers or their proxy systems), and management services (event filter agent). This interface is defined by the XMP (X-open management protocol) API. It is based on the consolidated management API specification of the OSF's DME API.

Management Platform Event Management Services. The EMS routes and logs events in a multivendor enterprise network. The EMS consists of two primary components, the event filter agent and the event log agent.

The event filter agent has two major functions. On a managed system, the filter agent forwards event reports from the generating system to the filter agent on the management stations. On the management station the filter agent delivers incoming event reports to any management application or agent that has registered for that event. In the case where the event is generated on a management station, as is the case for expert-system managed events as shown in Figure 4.6, both functions are performed by the local filter agent.

The event log is the repository for storing enterprise network events. The event log agent controls the event log. By default, the log agent could log all incoming events. The event log agent, like other management infrastructure applications and agents, registers an event filter with the event filter agent. Those events that pass the filter are forwarded to the event log agent, for recording the event log. Through the event log agent, management applications have programmatic access to the event log. This access provides applications a way to dynamically examine the history of events and apply filters to determine which events are to be logged or retrieved, to delete logged events, and to control the size of the event log. Using the programmatic access to the event log, applications will be created to provide event log interaction methods specific to the enterprise network management applications.

Enterprise Network Management Process. The management platform/server will provide the services necessary for layered management applications to communicate with network element managers (or their proxy systems). It should support the XMP to enable parallel development of management applications. The components of the management platform that are involved with the implementation of the network management process are very similar to those employed in the event process. The main difference is that in the case of the management process, applications have direct access to the communications infrastructure via the

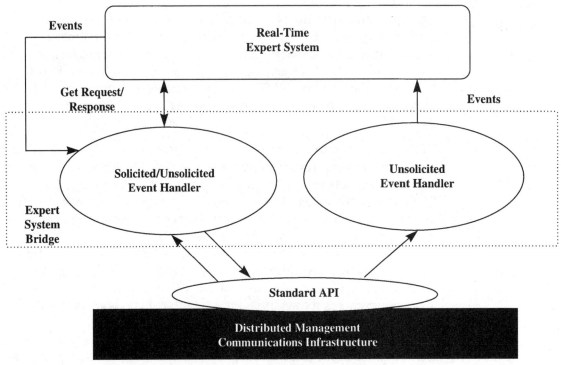

Figure 4.7   Expert System and Integrated Management Platform

XOM/XMP application programmers interface. This API provides access to the underlying network management protocols. Most off-the-shelf platform vendors support SNMP, CMIP, CMOL, and CMOT.

Expert System Server.   The integrated management of an enterprise network involves the use of a commercially available expert system to make decisions about alarms and messages in real time, based on the rules, procedures, object definitions, and relationships developed for the different enterprise services components. An off-the-shelf expert system shell is integrated into the overall enterprise network management platform, as shown in Figure 4.7. A bridge or an interface module could easily be developed between the management platform services and a third-party-provided expert system using the XOM/XMP application programmers interface.

Expert System Event Process.   Events are received by the management platform via its communications infrastructure. They are passed to the expert system bridge process through the use of the management platform's event management services. The bridge process should handle both unsolicited and solicited events for optimum performance.

Expert System Management Process. Based on the knowledge that has been encapsulated within the expert system, conclusions about alarm correlation and consolidation will be made and communicated via SNMP traps to the management server for further processing and operator interface, accordingly. The rules, procedures, and object definitions within the expert system along with the network topology will make the proper fault analysis and alarm correlation. Appropriate operator advice and/or automatic control will then be generated.

SUMMARY

Managing enterprise networks is a complex and challenging task. It must be carefully planned and its architecture must accommodate growth while providing increasing network reliability. In addition, a real-time integrated management system needs to keep pace with significant network events. The fastest such events are alarms, and the slowest are operator interventions. All occur asynchronously and unpredictably. Given the paradigm of management by exception, as discussed in earlier chapters, this could mean the rate of events being generated, from varying elements and their management systems, will be on the order of 100 per minute. Also, the integrated management system should have a strategy for handling an avalanche of events such as those caused by a significant failure, without simply giving up and failing at this crucial moment. It is extremely important to develop intermediate representation in order to handle such frequent events. Thus local filtering and automation (like application managers, element management systems, etc.), to the extent possible, can perform very temporal reasoning, and try to resolve the problem condition locally before passing them on to the integrated management system that has more reasoning capabilities based on its wide KB.

CHAPTER 5

Key Issues in Management of Networked Systems

Introduction

Managing globally distributed information networks is nontrivial and usually complex. These networked systems require a level of management aimed at reliable and cost-effective delivery of information and related services. Information network providers are measured by their ability to meet service-level agreements with their customers. Businesses recognize the inherent value of the information network as a competitive tool, and they require ways to capitalize on that asset. They need the flexibility to add new technology easily, to increase or decrease the scope of their networked systems quickly and efficiently, and to automate the many management tasks usually done manually.

Organizations' business depends on their ability to keep operational costs down while providing the highest possible levels of service and responsiveness, using different vendors' equipment. It is simply not enough to monitor network faults or gather performance data on each individual network component. It is extremely important to integrate management information at different levels of abstraction. Information is necessary to facilitate effective planning and design, performance trend analysis, and accounting or other administrative functions. Information networks require a means to manage service level agreements that measure the availability of mission-critical services and applications to their customers. Information networks offer an excellent opportunity to use a distributed, object-oriented approach as a means to this end. This type of approach enables multiple views of the same management information, permits easy introduction of new technologies and services, and makes possible the automation of most management tasks. It enables organizations to move towards a self-healing information network; in other words, it provides the end-users with a network dialtone at all times. This chapter will discuss some key issues and strategies for managing a distributed information network. The approach and emphasis will be on management services where traditional management functions (fault, performance, security, configuration, and accounting,) are horizontally integrated.

Networked System Model

Information networking services management environment (INSME) represents the amalgamation of the functions of operating and managing networked systems. The life cycle of an effective INSME strategy begins with designing and implementing an operations service architecture. The next step is to get the network under control and, finally, to optimize performance to mission-critical reliability. The first phase includes design and planning activities that include:

- identifying and establishing management services
- scale pricing and service levels agreements
- baseline performance level

The second phase includes operations such as FM and monitoring of networks and systems. This includes routine day-to-day operations and support services. Some functions that are typical of organizations are:

- maintenance
- network control center activities
- help desk

- network monitoring (availability and reliability)
- systems monitoring
- fault management
- configuration management
- change management
- asset management
- management applications integration

For organizations that migrated off the mainframe and have since gained experience in managing the distributed environment, management operations might be less problematic than for those that are currently making the transition. The third phase, managing the distributed systems (includes all networked elements and processes), optimizes the networked system with services like capacity planning and server workload management. A key challenge here would be in the execution of these services in heterogeneous environments.

When management of information networks is characterized by services, developing the processes for collecting service requirements, pricing products, monitoring service levels, and ultimately managing customer satisfaction is a difficult proposition. With a wide range of potential services, the temptation is to establish a standard (often large) service level agreement (SLA) to articulate the details. While a standard process for gathering the information and a standard method of articulating SLA details is paramount, users must develop manageable (brief and direct) documents that can be easily understood by the parties involved in service delivery, management, and reception. In some organizations, service level tracking and reporting is now the purview of the new enterprise service desk (an integrated customer and network support center).

Managing information networks encompasses a variety of issues associated with designing the network, operating the network, and identifying problems in the network when an error condition occurs. Due to the challenges involved in managing such a network, it offers a wide range of opportunities to apply evolving and leading edge technologies.

For discussion purposes, the management framework described here assumes a large globally distributed information network. As these networks grow in complexity and size, feature and service requirements expand, and new information technologies are introduced—all at an increasing rate—the systems that manage and operate such a network become complex. The management framework described will be based on an architecture that segments the network into elements, element management systems (EMS), and an integrating management platform to tie it all together, providing complete end-to-end visibility, control, and status across domains, functions, processes, systems, and services.

The challenges of intelligent management of information networks is managing the business applications and its associated processing systems, along with the other traditional data communication and networking elements. This involves managing the various distributed applications, different gateways, information traffic, routing tables, special services, and other unique characteristics and peculiarities of a specific organization's network and correlating their behavior with other events and alarms that are generated by the rest of the network.

A fundamental approach in intelligent management of information networks is to carefully characterize different problem conditions associated with underlying mission-critical and noncritical application and appropriately address their resolution locally to the extent possible, and blend the approach with an expert system based problem resolver, for recovering from complicated problems or problems that require a higher level of reasoning and correlation of multiple seemingly disparate problem conditions.

For illustration purposes, it is assumed that an information network model consists of three classes of elements: access/egress network, backbone transport network, and systems and applications. Figure 5.1 depicts an example of a networked system model. In addition, an operations and management environment from which the entire network is normally managed is assumed to be part of the overall networked system model.

Access Network

The function of the access network is to connect the end-user with a processing node (a host computer) where the requested information service is available. The access network often uses a LAN or WAN so it is publicly accessible from any location, although other methods of access, such as packet, are also provided. In addition, the access network will be responsible for dialing out of the information network depending on the various delivery options chosen by the end-user. Typical access network elements are facilities, multiplexers, demultiplexers, modems, etc. Usually, these network elements have some sort of management capabilities that are integrated within those elements, or else they are standalone element management systems.

Figure 5.1
Example of a
Networked System
Model

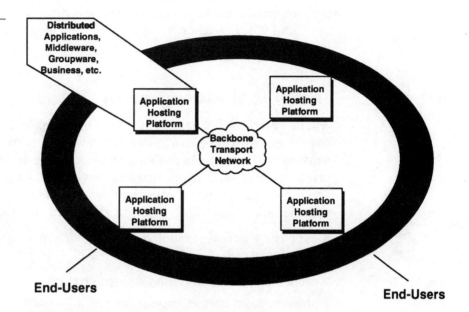

Backbone Transport Network

The backbone data transport network provides connectivity between the processing nodes. It allows information transaction to be routed from one node to another and allows nodes to share control information. The backbone transport network is utilized for several back-end functions like authentication, security, routing table changes, load balancing, information transport to a local node, etc. Typical backbone transport networking elements consists of routers, LAN hubs, high-speed trunks, switches, etc. Typically these WAN or backbone transport network components have some capabilities in their system for management and control functions and some of these WAN elements even provide standalone element management systems with interfaces to standard and popular integrated management systems.

Applications and Systems

The application systems in an information network have two functions: they engage in a session with the end-user that allows the initiation and execution of a business or other service transaction, and they perform back-end processing to route transactions to other processing systems and network end points. For our modeling and design purposes, it is assumed that the information network consists of several processing systems distributed across the globe. This is desirable if disaster recovery is of importance and also if access costs have to be kept to a minimum (especially important in a global network).

Integrated Management

A true enterprise management environment must be able to perform centralized, distributed, or hybrid management of the distributed networking environment in a homogeneous manner. It must accommodate private, public, and virtual network services for data, image, and voice applications, requiring a consistent set of integrated and coordinated tools. Some key operations/functions/management tasks include:

- problem detection, isolation, and resolution
- problem reporting and tracking
- work order coordination and resource tracking
- inventory and asset management
- service cost estimating
- end-to-end PM of business-specific transactions and reporting
- chargeback and billing management
- service-level agreement and management
- CM
- SM
- consolidation and standardization of operator/user interface

As is evident, some of the management functions described above extend beyond traditional network management theories. They include functions normally associated with telemanagement, physical management systems, and network service management. For discussion purposes, the following definitions will be used to characterize the element management systems, domain management systems and enterprise (or integrated) management systems. EMSs monitor and, to some extent, control the various devices within the networked environment. An element is defined as any network or system device with diagnostic capabilities, including modems, multiplexers, applications, systems, etc. Domain management systems are higher-level element managers. Domain management refers to the ability to work within specific domains, such as the SNA network, voice network, messaging networks, internet/intranet, or an individual LAN. Enterprise (or integrated) management systems incorporate domain and element management for all networks within the enterprise. An enterprise represents the sum total of an organization, where all its operating units are viewed as one collective body. It may include subsidiaries, affiliates, suppliers, and customers.

Key Operations Management Services

Managing an information network includes managing all the components discussed in earlier sections, and presenting the integrated results in a way that enhances the operability of the network. The idea is to collect all status reports and alarm conditions, no matter what type of equipment or software subsystem they come from, and present network operations and management center with only the most useful and urgent information that is beyond the capabilities of the local element management system. Some automation using an expert system might filter incoming alarms and events, take automatic corrective action, and give detailed advice based on the history and KB.

Monitoring and keeping track of all the bits and pieces, nodes and workstations, black boxes and connecting devices, and application servers and systems that make up a network-centric computing environment is nontrivial. Identifying trouble spots and handling all the administrative chores generated by an ever-growing, ever-changing end-user population make it all the more difficult. What is needed is automated help in the form of a management control system. The primary goal of such a system is quite simple: to identify and replace the faulty element, but to achieve this nirvana is quite a challenge.

Consider a data path, for example. A user's personal computer might pass information to a network adapter card, then over a LAN to a communications server, and then to a router that uses a broadband backbone network, just to reach a front-end processor that sends information to an application server. And the returning data has to retrace those steps. Problems can occur anywhere along this path, and the range of possible problems is wide. Finding a single management system capable of doing the entire job is next to impossible, if not cost prohibitive. However, some new-generation management platforms enable one to integrate systems that can gather data from a variety of third-party applications and present it in a consistent interface.

Organizations should take both strategic and tactical steps to control their distributed information networks. At its core, defining and selecting a management platform is crucial as it provides important benefits: first, a base level of interoperability between multivendor applications and services; second, a level playing field for management application development through the provision of common application programming interfaces. The platform infrastructure should be architected such that it provides a method for legacy systems integration, the filtering/correlation/automation engine, an object and database strategy, management protocol support, and platform scalability. The platform should be standardized at both enterprise and domain levels.

Monitoring

The monitoring of networks and systems is the foundation upon which all of network operations is built. It provides automated discovery and mapping of the network, and prioritizes events gathered from anywhere in the networking environment. Instrumenting the networks and systems is critical for monitoring the services. Hence both custom and standard software and hardware must be appropriately instrumented so that they generate sufficient warnings or alerts if something should go wrong or if there is degradation in networking services.

Fault Management Services

FM is the detection, diagnosis, and resolution of network and system failures on a remote basis. Nodes can be monitored proactively or reactively. Critical network components are actively monitored by probes or traps with defined threshold conditions to prevent failures or performance losses. When an alarm condition is detected, FM tools and procedures are used to restore the alarming component to its normal state. Standard protocols used in FM include SNMP and remote monitoring (RMON). These standards should be supplemented by proprietary extensions. One function of the tools is maintaining and analyzing problem resolution history to create new automatic problem resolution rules. Another function is the automated generation of trouble tickets.

True management of a networking environment requires both solicited and unsolicited events to help detect abnormal conditions. Usually the problem is that too many events are generated in an unsolicited manner. If these are not appropriately filtered, network operators become hopelessly overloaded. The first step is the elimination of irrelevant alerts. The second step is to put together related management information to define specific network events. Finally, events should be assigned priorities and thresholds. Threshold violations and events of certain priorities should trigger alarms.

The alarms generation process is accomplished in a networked computing environment by local application managers, device managers, and associated element management systems. Depending on the complexity and size of the information network, event management can become a very extensive activity. Usually fault management is the most complex of all the management applications and is also closely tied to the management platform infrastructure. In addition, event and alarm condition logging is necessary for record keeping and diagnostic purposes, for reviewing events that occurred during unattended mode of operation, and above all to build the knowledge and history base for the expert system. A model to design this application will be explored in detail in this section.

Very often FM is confused with PM. It is important to note that what has been discussed so far in regard to detecting, isolating, and resolving faults is different from resolving those faults in terms of escalation procedures, trouble reporting, and ticketing. In effect, FM is the process of keeping an information services network operational. PM as a database application automates the reporting and tracking of information network problems.

Fault Management Service Architecture.   One of the most challenging aspects of FM is alarm/event correlation, consolidation, and problem isolation. To be able to correlate events in a distributed information networking environment, it is necessary for the application to access management information about the network. In reality, this information is contained in varying formats, and distributed among heterogeneous network resources. By designing and developing a generic managed object model, the integrated management system can be freed from dependency on diverse network resources. In a generic model, similar attributes are used by the integrated management system in a homogeneous fashion for managed objects representing the information services network.

A generic model of an information services network makes provision for physical and logical views of the network. It should contain sufficient information to describe the network in terms of systems, communication entities, physical links, and logical connections. The expert system that is part of the overall integrated management system will play a key role in correlating events and providing resolution techniques based on the history, KB, and current status of the information network. In order to develop this FM application, it is essential to understand an important aspect of it, namely, correlation. Alarm correlation is becoming extremely important in effectively managing large distributed information networks. The three most important features in the expert-system-based FM of information networks are the event processor, relationship exploration, and correlation and causality.

The expert system for the most part is passive until an event arrives. Then the correlation engine of the expert system should start processing the event immediately. As a result, the FM model is driven by incoming events and works on a dynamic information base, where events are added during the process of correlation (the expert system switching between solicited and unsolicited/solicited mode of operation, on demand). The expert system runs continuously as long as events arrive, and it will attempt to correlate them to other events in the database.

The expert system correlates events by detecting special relationships between the source objects of those events. Usually, in a distributed information services network, only a small part of the information required to establish these relationships is included in the event reports themselves. Therefore, for each incoming event, the application sends requests to the SNMP agents (or to the proxy SNMP agent, as described in the previous chapter) in order to collect information about other objects with which it is in relationship. The correlation engine then proceeds, based on this information, which is maintained in the MIB. However, in the presence of several failures, parts of the network may not be reachable either directly or through the proxy agent, causing requests to time out. In order to avoid these excessive delays, the exploration of the various objects should be accomplished in parallel. This involves innovative ways of using the SNMP protocol and the associated MIB (demand polling, exception based event processing, etc.).

It is important to determine what has to be correlated before the mechanism of correlation itself is discussed. The expert system that is being described for FM is aimed at the processing of events that indicate a failure or other nonnormal condition, such as unreachable node, queue buildup, etc. The objective of correlation is to identify event reports that occur as symptoms of the same fault. A few key relationships are identified, which have proved to be important for describing fault propagation and, therefore, for event correlation.

One underlying assumption is that faults often occur in lower layers of the information services communication architecture (e.g., message handler, message transport, or hardware level), thereby causing side effects in higher layers (e.g., queue buildup, service gateway congestion, or information corruption). Thus, one direction to search for the cause of an event is downward. Another important search direction is horizontally, i.e., between connections of the same layer. Two nodes may be coupled, e.g., at the router or at a gateway level. When a link in one of the nodes fails, connections in both networks will experience outages or through-put degrades resulting in traffic congestion and queue backup. It is to be noted that downward search may not yield any result in the node that is operating normally, since the source of the problem is in the other node. The sympathy events from the two nodes can only be correlated at the layer of the communication architecture at which the two nodes are interconnected. This is accomplished only via a horizontal search.

Using these guidelines, it is extremely important to develop relationships between different managed objects in the information services network. Since different information services utilize different resources and underlying core services, careful planning should go into the development of the relationships. Over time the expert system should gather information to be used in the correlation task by exploring the relationships for the source object, and for the managed objects related to that object.

Exploration for received events takes place in parallel by using a mechanism in which for each new incoming event a different search activity is initiated to find the managed objects related to the source object instance. New search activities are also started for each new object discovered in this way. This process continues until no more unexplored objects can be discovered. It is critical to develop correct relationships between different managed objects and then to build the KB for real-time inferencing by the expert system. The overall design approach described makes it possible for the expert fault management system to retrieve all the necessary relationships via attributes of generic managed objects.

The management traffic that could potentially be generated as a result of the dynamic exploration of relationships through the retrieval of managed object attribute values could place an additional load on the network. This could be optimized by exploring relationships using static configuration information where this is available (e.g., information stored in the CMIR), thus only accessing the information network when the information is not readily available in local storage.

Thus, an accurate representation of the information network topology is crucial if real-time correlation and inferencing is to be achieved.

This could be accomplished by close coupling with a relational database-driven physical network management application. All moves, adds, and changes are to be accurately recorded and immediately made available for all the management applications to update their respective databases. Hence it is critical that organizations develop a CMIR irrespective of the management platforms, applications, and tools being used. This will significantly reduce the load in terms of dynamic exploration of the relationships between different managed objects over the management network.

Fault isolation involves two basic steps: event correlation and causality decision. Event correlation decides whether two events result from the same primary information network component failure. Causality decision involves determining whether one of the failures indicated by two correlated events caused the other, i.e., whether one of the two lies close to the source of the failure. It is to be noted that the correlation step does not make any statement about causality. It only determines whether the two events belong together irrespective of their cause.

The relationship exploration discussed previously provides the necessary information to the expert system to enable it to decide whether two events are correlated. If, during a search activity resulting from a given event, a relationship is discovered to an object that is already known to the application as a result of a search activity investigating a different event, the two events are regarded as correlated. The actions to be taken once it has been decided that two events are correlated are significantly influenced by assumptions about the nature of the correlation and rules that have been put in the KB. It is to be noted that two events are correlated if they result from the same failure. Correlation does not include any information about causality.

Taking correlation as an equivalency relation, the FM is simplified. The set of all events should be partitioned into sets containing correlated events or event sets. Any one event belongs to exactly one event set, which may as an extreme case be a set containing only this one event. When it has been ascertained as a result of exploration that two events from different event sets are correlated, then all events included in the two sets are correlated. With this model, the correlation process becomes straightforward.

■ For each incoming event, an event set containing only this event is created.

■ The exploration process is started for the event and a search tree is built using the object instance relationships mentioned earlier. When at least one common object instance is discovered, the two events are correlated.

■ When two events from different event sets are correlated, the two event sets are merged.

Although the grouping of related events (consolidation and correlation) is extremely helpful to the network operator, it still does not provide more information about the source of the failure. Hence the expert FM application should continue to establish, where possible, an *ordering* among the events within the same event set, where the ordering indicates which event is most closely related to the source of the failure and which ones resulted as a sympathy to that failure. This ordering represents a directed relationship among correlated events, *causality.* It constitutes a first step at fault isolation and directs further diagnostic and testing activities in the right direction. The fault resolution is achieved based on the rules established in the expert system.

The expert FM application is information networking environment specific. The knowledge engineers must supply exhaustive operational and facility information from both the network operator's and the end-user's perspective to define workable rules and develop a comprehensive KB. It is important to correctly model the fault notification, isolation, correlation, and recovery procedures. The FM application implemented without these prerequisites seldom achieves its objectives and/or its full potential.

Fault Management Services Summary

In the expert FM application described in this section, a major assumption is that the network consists of EMSs, and that there are several legacy systems that require the use of a proxy server for using a standard management information communication protocol (SNMP). The straightforward case of all standard systems will be a simpler realization of this approach. In addition, the FM application is described based on the fact that an integrated management system is the recipient of all filtered information network events. The primary role of any integrated management system will be to ensure the correct operation of the information network. Its role is to correct a problem when it occurs, thus requiring the identification of the cause of the fault, the isolation of its origin, the repair of the component, and the restoration of the information service to its normal operational status. The FM application model, as described previously in this section, helps in realizing these objectives.

The incomplete nature of the information that is made available to the integrated management system, the overlapping views provided by the individual EMSs, and the context-sensitive nature of FM in an information network, strongly justifies the use of a real-time expert system. To support an architecture of open interfaces to the integrated information network management infrastructure, the design approach described is intended to support vendor-neutral components and management applications.

Configuration Management Services

CM and physical management of information networks are closely related functions that are absolutely necessary for managing the information services network that utilizes an expert system in the integrated management platform. Most management systems primarily focus on FM, relying on manual physical topology and configuration information. Most often, these manual techniques fail to accurately reflect what is in the information network, much less the relationships between the various managed objects. This is particularly true of large global networks built using multivendor components and devices.

In large public information networks, resources and configuration information, such as routing tables, change periodically. Several of these changes are not documented or are not coordinated (especially in a distributed management environment) by the central network management and control authority. Without adequate physical network and configuration management controls, it is virtually impossible to effectively realize any other management application (e.g., FM). To build a comprehensive integrated information network management infrastructure, it is evident that interoperability has multiple dimensions, loosely divided into two components: managing the logical side of networks and managing the information network's physical infrastructure.

Configuration (or physical) management involves tracking the network infrastructure and its connectivity. While inventory (or asset) management documents network resources, configuration management is a more dynamic process, describing the state and parameters of these resources. Configuration management includes setting parameters and changing the state of a managed object. An information network's configuration is typically described in terms of physical connections (like circuits and routers) and logical connections (like core information services and applications). Configuration management may also keep track of how the network is connected either temporally or based on geography of the nodes, information functions. Inventory and configuration management often overlap in real-world applications, as inventory records can contain entries for end-point connections, hierarchy, etc.

The widespread focus and attention towards management information protocol standards, performance, and management applications—all elements of logical network management—often eclipse the increasing complexity and importance of the physical infrastructure and its management issues. One of the biggest challenges in effectively managing an information network is to develop a workable methodology that will let the network operators solve both physical and logical networking issues, and integrate them with existing management tools.

Physical (or configuration) network management is today's missing link for overall end-to-end integrated management of information networks. Most enterprises already manage their networks using a variety of tools that monitor traffic, identify node failures, and manage other logically related and connected elements. Although these logical network management tools are very valuable in tracking the logical connections of intelligent network devices, they do not track the details of the infrastructure.

Today, there is no single system that can solve both logical and physical network management issues. However, the market requirement for an integrated solution to both sides of the network management framework has led many vendors to create open systems that can be linked together to form a comprehensive integrated management system.

Integrated management of an information system requires a set of tools that address and improve these key functionalities: managing the logical components of the network, managing the information network's physical infrastructure, and managing the requests to effect changes to either or both of the network's logical and/or physical components. The reason for these functionalities is that with any logical network management system, the operator is notified of a problem in the network via an alert mechanism but is not given information regarding the location or the identity of the network component that sent the alert. Furthermore, there is no provision for generating a trouble ticket (automatic or manual) to ensure that the problem gets tracked and resolved in a timely manner.

In an INMS, when a problem is identified, the system itself creates and automatically dispatches the trouble ticket to resolve the problem. This is done after extensive interaction with the expert system to ascertain the nature of the actual problem and after correlating with other problems and/or trouble tickets related to this problem. The ticket automatically includes physical location information, work history, asset information, and an end-to-end circuit trace showing all the physical components that could be affecting this failure. In the case of software components, the system points to the exact information service or its component that is experiencing an outage or problem.

In addition to providing configuration information, the INMS provides connectivity management information. This is extremely important in an information network that is globally distributed with distributed control. This system provides the operator with a graphical document of the physical locations of all networking equipment (WAN components), including hubs, routers, patch panels, switches, etc. This system also provides connectivity information, such as port configurations, circuits lists, and routing tables. The connectivity of all of these items must be tracked, maintained, and available online for immediate and real-time access from a standard presentation interface.

This level of detail and flexibility allows information service providers and network managers to efficiently design, manage, maintain, and install different information services with ease. It is essential to integrate all the physical drawings with a standard relational database management system so that they are linked to textual information regarding the network topology. The dynamic link between graphics and the database ensures that changes made in one format are automatically updated in the other, so that information is always current and reliable. Linking the logical management capabilities with physical topology or configuration information along with an expert system, the network operators have access to a dynamic, real-time correlation between seemingly different problem conditions and problem resolution techniques. A step further could automate this process, with just an event report to the operator of the various actions taken by the integrated management system. This type of correlation, along with the approaches described in the previous section, provides a means to solve information network problems more quickly, and minimize downtime, and improve network reliability and diagnostic and repair activities.

Another important aspect of integrated management is the link between the logical/physical management and trouble-ticketing capabilities, as discussed before. This section will briefly discuss some architectural and design issues as part of the overall integrated management platform. Defining a process for timely resolution of problems and support requests is a challenge. As part of the integrated management infrastructure, a problem resolution system along with associated management process provides a flexible, customizable work flow process for both network operators and other support staff. One objective for this integrated management system is to reduce the time and cost associated with issuing, tracking, and resolving network problems and network change requests.

A carefully designed integrated management infrastructure provides a centralized source of information for network problem resolution as well as a work flow process for dispatching and effecting change. For instance, network engineering staff will be able to submit network and/or service change requests using a standard set of forms that is driven off of the configuration management application, which automatically includes user information and details about the device's actual location, or existing network topology, as well as an end-to-end circuit trace showing the device's connectivity. A predefined (or by operator override) work flow process automatically validates the trouble report with the expert system to verify its authenticity, correlate with other similar problem conditions, and then route the ticket appropriately. While the management of trouble tickets, work orders, and change requests appears to be simplistic, providing a means of automating and efficiently managing all of the various requests and providing a timely resolution are a key component to an integrated management of information services network.

Configuration Management Summary.   Change management encompasses the introduction, tracking, and measurement of modifications to hardware, software, network, and system technology. One component, physical inventory, entails the maintenance of configuration parameters on network devices such as hubs, routers, bridges, servers, and workstations. This is partially achieved through automated scanning of MIB files. The balance is achieved with proprietary tools and/or processes. A second component of CM concerns moves, adds, and changes. The tracking of desktop equipment, network addresses, software (both standard and custom), and telecommunications must be centralized and, optimally, updated in real time for use by others. Finally, software version control and user login rights are both important pieces of configuration management, though closely related to other system management functions. The goal of configuration management is to keep the network, servers, system components, and user profiles current and documented.

Capacity and Performance Management Services

PM capabilities include mechanisms to monitor and analyze the performance of the managed network and its associated information services. Results of performance analysis may trigger diagnostic testing procedures as well as initiate configuration changes in order to maintain the prescribed level of service or performance. Performance management provides procedures to collect and disseminate data concerning the current state of the information network, and maintain and analyze performance logs along with service level objectives and predefined metrics.

An important aspect that needs to be thought through is the calculation of performance metrics: should the calculation be performed by the agent or by the manager (integrated manager)? An integrated management platform, as described thus far, is the management system that lets network operators, managers, and analysts monitor, control, and test manageable objects in the information services network. An agent is the management software that provides a remote management interface to the managed object. It provides information about the object's internal state through traps and events, and provides a means for manipulating the services and devices the object supports. Thus the agent is the source of observed management data. In addition, the majority of the performance data are being collected in existing information networks in various forms and places throughout the network and it is the intention of the integrated management system to provide a common means of collecting those metrics and develop a performance management model. Hence, for the information services network, it is recommended that the performance computation be done on the integrated management system.

Different aspects of performance management are usually performed by various management applications within an integrated management infrastructure. For example, the FM application provides the capability to set thresholds and identify conditions that constitute unacceptable performance levels, in the form of rules, and to provide unsolicited reporting when such thresholds are violated. It is also essential that there be a mechanism to export the performance data that is collected to a relational data base. This historical data is used to track the performance of the information network over time, and to do trend analysis. Other management applications within the integrated management platform utilize the performance data to do network tuning and optimization, including correlation of network events by the expert system.

Some key functional requirements for the performance management application are: performance event monitoring, identifying performance thresholds, performance analysis, control, and administration. Performance event monitoring facilities provide real-time monitoring of management data and the filtering of all nonperformance-related information. The performance analysis facilities provide for the collection of metrics from the managed objects that make up the information services network. In addition, it provides a means for creating and maintaining a historical database of performance statistics for the managed objects while analyzing the current performance statistics to detect faults. It is also essential to correlate the current statistics with historical data to predict long-term trends.

The PM application computes performance statistics for different information services and entities in a multivendor network. Some of the metrics are: alarm count, traffic volume, availability and reliability of the network, speed of service, accessibility of the network, call completion ratio, message volume based on type of message, and WAN statistics. The performance statistics are defined by formulae which require raw data over a time period as well as some specific characteristics regarding the information services and associated networking devices.

The criteria for managing the performance of an information network may be different for different user communities. It is essential to capture the three categories of the performance of the information network that deal with the end-users of the network, the managers of the network, and the designers of the network. Since information networks deal with different and mixed types of traffic, and vary in communications protocol, switching technique, grade of service, and type of information services, the performance management application will vary depending on the specific types of networks. Since this book deals with a practical approach to managing an existing information services network, we will only deal with designing the PM application based on measurements and not by simulation or analytical approaches.

Performance Metrics Agents for Information Networks. Performance metrics measurement agents play an important role in the integrated management of information networks and it is important to find a way to integrate them into the overall management framework. Since most of the management function in a standards-based approach (SNMP) is achieved using an object database (MIB), it is obvious that the performance metrics will also be measured and reported based on this approach. The MIB is an external representation of management information stored in the managed system. When remote applications wish to change the behavior of a system they manage, they manipulate the MIB values, using a remote operations protocol (SNMP primitives). Changes to the MIB effect changes in the operation of the remote system.

As an example, consider retrieving a routing table from a remote switch. This retrieval is accomplished by sending a query that requests the routing table stored in the MIB. The switch will return a copy of the routing table as it is stored in the MIB. The actual routing table in the switch is usually in an entirely different format from the one presented in the MIB. The MIB representation is simply an external view of the routing data that all managed objects (or systems) must support. The managed object is responsible for converting from this internal format to the external MIB format expected by the PM application in the integrated management system. As discussed in previous chapters, the entity on the managed system that does this conversion is called an *agent*. This agent could be an SNMP agent or a proxy SNMP agent for systems that do not support standard management information communication protocol such as SNMP.

The easiest way to represent a measurement agent in a MIB is to define a set of objects that represents a measurement activity associated with one or more performance metrics. In particular, this activity is a set of objects that models the measurement program being run, the output being generated by that program, and any controls or constraints that one wishes to apply to the program or its output. Hence, a significant effort has to be put into defining the MIB associated with performance metrics and the means of obtaining the information with minimal SNMP queries.

Performance Metrics Requirements.   The requirements for a comprehensive and composite report on a regular basis (determined by local needs) are listed below. It is important that the data collection and processing be based on a common time zone, especially when the information network is globally distributed. The performance metrics are grouped into three main categories: availability, reliability, and serviceability.

Availability.   Availability of an information service from an end-user's perspective is a combination of several factors. A set of metrics are to be defined and measured in the following ways.

- Identify the components involved in the end-user's access to the information services network.
- Identify scheduled and unscheduled outages for the various information network components (both software and hardware).
- Define the end-user outage time metric for all the elements in the network by identifying failures, causes, and their effects, and map them into network elements; then derive end-user outage time and quantify them in terms of number of user sessions interrupted or information service being unavailable, and assign appropriate weights.

In effect, this type of measurement takes an inside-out approach (as opposed to treating the information network as a black box and measuring customer availability from outside) and provides customer availability data and identifies component level failures and their causes. This approach helps in identifying the degree by which each of these components contribute to the unavailability of the information network from an end-user's perspective. It is extremely important to track and manage these metrics.

Reliability.   Information network reliability, from an end-user's perspective, is defined as to whether the network is doing what the customer expects it to do. This includes metrics like mailbox-to-mailbox delivery time, delivery of messages to the end-point within the preset service level objective, and speed of service. These metrics could be different for different types of information services like video, voice, interactive multimedia, fax, X.400, EDI, etc.

Serviceability.   Serviceability is also sometimes termed *operability of the network*. This is usually the measure by which the network operations can service the network easily and bring the affected service back online before the end-users notice any major degradation of service. Serviceability could include such metrics as the number of alarms the network operators have to respond to or take action on, the number of corrupted messages (dead letter) requiring human intervention, etc.

An important aspect of PM of information services networks is developing a framework for measuring and managing the three major metrics (others could be derivatives of one of the three) by identifying what the end-user wants, establishing a set of measures that addresses those wants, and tracking the measures to see how well the network is performing. Once these measures are defined and a continuous measurement process is put in place, the resulting data is used to identify inherent problems in the network for improvement. Figure 5.2 describes these metrics from both an end-user and a network provider's perspective.

Performance Management Services Summary.   PM optimizes response times between critical components within a networking environment. Critical components could include routers, application servers, mainframe hosts, access/egress infrastructure, and backbone transport connections. Performance management consists of three areas: monitoring, analysis, and capacity planning. Monitoring and analysis are the process of identifying bottlenecks in network operations. This is typically achieved by periodically sending packets from one router to another and capturing the average time elapsed. Corrective measures may then dictate bringing down network servers to refresh system files, or upgrading server memory or storage. Proactive monitoring ensures that problems are handled before users are impacted. Capacity planning is understanding the workload an element is carrying at any

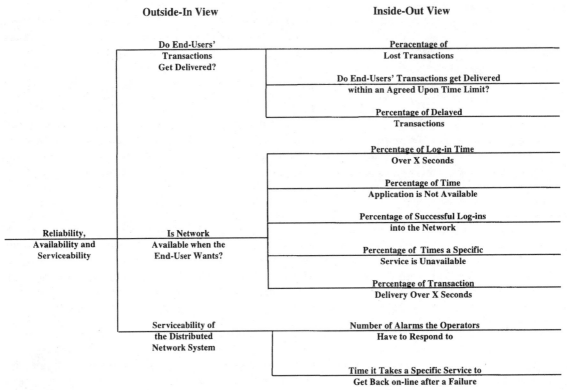

Figure 5.2 Performance Metrics Model for Distributed Networked System Environment

given moment, and predicting how a network will perform under greater loads in the future. Network modeling costs tools can be used to develop alternate scenarios for network traffic loads.

Service Level Agreements

Since the management of an information networking environment is a business within a business, it is important that a well-defined set of metrics be developed and a level of service agreed upon as part of the overall management of the networked system environment. SLAs are not a new concept, but many organizations have been reluctant to develop them because they require significant time investments. Without SLAs, user organizations may have no idea whether the service providing organization is improving service, whether the chargebacks are appropriate, or even what service the organization is providing at all. SLAs are more prevalent in organizations that use external service providers (outsourcing) for their networking services. It is critical that organizations adopt such best practices for internal measurements as well, as these practices are bound to help an organization continuously improve their quality of service and more importantly focus on services as opposed to merely on technology.

An SLA is a contract between the service provider and the end-user, and should be employed regardless of whether the provider is internal or external. Internal IT groups will find SLAs to be effective tools for justifying added value in the face of external competition. When designed jointly with end-users, SLAs are a powerful aid in assuring customer input to IT planning, supporting chargeback administration, and providing a measurable base for IT performance. SLAs build on the foundation laid by the initial service definitions as discussed earlier in this chapter. Some core components of the SLA are:

- statement of objectives
- definition of terms
- listing of services (measurable events)
- responsibilities of service center organization (help desk, network control center, maintenance, etc.)
- end-user responsibilities
- service coverage
- response time categories
- chargeback process
- problem resolution, with remedies for failed performance
- metrics

It is important to note that SLAs are not merely numbers, such as 99.999 percent availability, without analyzing the underlying component for which availability is being defined. End-users must understand the correlation between expectations and cost. For example, certain end-users want 100 percent availability on WAN, LAN, and transaction servers, while in most cases practical acceptability level is about 99 percent. Incrementally, the cost of adding 1 percent on the margin can add 100 to 200 percent to the per-transaction costs.

End-users and service providers have to discuss SLAs rationally, given that the whole notion of service levels can be foreign to many users. The more sophisticated IT users apparently understand it in principle, but do not institute procedures to flesh out the details. For example, measuring 99 percent reliability/availability on servers should reflect extensive discussions between provider and user, employing a triage process for measuring loads, capacity, uptime, and so on.

As another example, in the help-desk scenario, all four of the following elements must be measured and reflected in the SLA:

- queue time
- first-level resolution time (e.g., dispatching)
- time to get someone on-site or working the problem off-site or online
- actual resolution time

Application-related SLAs are very hard to articulate and implement. On the problem side, it is easy to log trouble calls, schedule maintenance, forecast root-cause problem resolution times, and the like. It is relatively simple to put in service levels through level-two help. However, it is not as easy in the application/solutions development environment. For example, capturing business needs and tying them to development schedules and deliverables is still an art form. This is especially the case in client/server implementations, when the number of components needed to complete a transaction increases geometrically. Plans are affected continually by shifting business conditions, market and industry changes, enhancements to software, versioning, and releases tied to user needs.

One size SLA does not fit all. SLAs enable the user to continuously improve, in some cases to hold steady, and in other cases to reduce operating costs. For example, in the WAN, a lot is tied up in the carrier cost for the enterprise networked environment. The need for redundancies goes down as the equipment gets more reliable. The user must understand that 99.95 percent availability is adequate and that the marginal benefit of another redundant router is low. Figures 5.3, 5.4, 5.5, 5.6, 5.7 and 5.8 describe some typical metrics to develop and measure for a distributed systems environment.

Systems and Applications Management

Fundamentally, there are two distinct methods of detecting faults in a networked system environment: proactive and reactive. The proactive method is enabled by instrumenting the target elements (system or appli-

Figure 5.3
Metrics and Service
Level Management
Approach

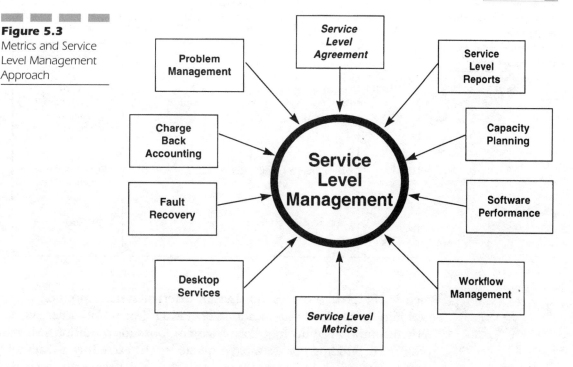

cations as the case may be). The reactive method is merely capturing
events and alerts that are generated by inherent capabilities of those ele-

Figure 5.4
Sample Metrics for
End-User Support
Services

Process	Components That Form Measurement	Metrics
Help Desk	Level 1 will be resolved on first contact. Level 2 will be those requiring routing calls to specialists. Customer Satisfaction	82% - Level 1 18% - Level 2 100% Goal
Resolution	Call placed on hold Time calls placed on hold Calls routed correctly Number of re-works Customer Satisfaction	<10% 95% <2 minutes 100% <1 per month 100% Goal

Figure 5.5
Sample Metrics for
Training Services

Process	Components That Form Measurement	Metrics
Training	Percentage of end-users trained Post-course instructor performance ratings by students	95% utilized 4.2 of possible 5.0 effectiveness measurement
	Date of training certification issued	<30 days of course completion
	Customer Satisfaction	100% Goal

ments. The proactive method uses an external system monitor, which periodically checks the applications, operating system, and other system-related conditions. This monitoring system looks for conditions where a problem is building (for example, a queue length exceeding a threshold, traffic congestion, and so on) but a fault has not necessarily occurred.

Figure 5.6
Sample Metrics for
Telecommunications
Services

Process	Components That Form Measurement	Metrics
Telecommunications	Availability Level Scheduled maintenance outages	99.89% 10 per year not to exceed 6 hours

Voice	Line availability
	Routine moves, adds, and changes
	Directory accuracy
	New/upgrade service
	  1-5 Telephone units
	  6-20
	  >20
	  Telephone circuits inter establishment,
	  city or region (US)
	  Telephone circuits international
	
	Customer Satisfaction
		99.99%
		<5 working days
		98%
		5 working days
		7 working days
		12 per week
		17 work days
		60 work days
		
		90 work days
		
		100% Goal

Data	Availability Response time Resolution New/upgrade service Customer Satisfaction	24x7 <2 hour <30 min......... 14 days 100% Goal

Process	Components That Form Measurement	Metrics
Desktops (PC/Workstations)		
New acquisitions and/or upgrades	Number requiring re-work Acquisition/Installation	< 2% 4 days to release the purchase order, 2 days from receipt to installation
	Customer Satisfaction	100% Goal
Relocation	Number requiring re-work Delivered on schedule	< 1% 100% Goal
	Customer satisfaction	100% Goal
Maintenance - *Mission Critical*	Mission critical equipment will be identified by customer. Assume 10% of installation base. Number requiring re-work	4 hours response, 8 hours return to service < 1%
- *Non-critical*	All equipment not listed as critical Number requiring re-work Customer Satisfaction	8 hours response, 24 hours return to service < 2% 100% Goal

Figure 5.7   Sample Metrics for Desktop Related Services

This application manager also usually has provision to automatically take corrective action, locally, in response to certain potential problem condi-

Figure 5.8   Sample Service Level Report

SLA#	SLA Description	Min%	Current Month(CM)	CM-1	CM-2	CM-3	# Missed Last 10 Months
1.1	*Platform Availability*						
1.1.1	NT Systems	99.0%	99.7%	99.7%	99.3%	99.4%	0
1.1.3	VAX Systems 3 of 3	99.0%	100.0%	99.8%	99.5%	99.7%	0
1.1.4	Unix Servers 37 of 37	99.8%	99.9%	99.8%	99.7%	99.9%	0
1.2	*Network Availability*						
1.2.1	SNA	99.0%	100.0%	100.0%	100.0%	99.6%	0
1.2.2	TCP/IP Backbone 44 of 44	99.0%	99.9%	99.4%	99.7%	99.3%	0
1.2.3	Dialup Support	98.0%	99.9%	100.0%	100.0%	100.0%	0
1.3	*Applications Availability*						
1.3.1	Office Vision	98.5%	99.4%	99.7%	98.6%	99.4%	0
1.3.3	DBS Applications	98.5%	99.4%	99.2%	99.4%	98.7%	0
1.3.5	Order Entry	98.0%	99.0%	98.1%	98.8%	98.3%	0
1.3.6	Accounting	98.0%	98.5%	99.4%	99.3%	88.9%	2
1.4	*Output Availability*						
1.4.1	Production Job Output	99.0%	NA	NA	NA		

tions. Typically, in a distributed system environment, these are the types of faults that should be addressed and resolved locally in the system itself by adopting the above strategy.

Application management is a logical extension of the enterprise management approach because it focuses on the mission-critical applications that perform the core business functions of the enterprise. Like the network and system management functions, its operation is evaluated, coordinated, and enhanced by the expert system within the enterprise management infrastructure. Application management systems are intelligent, agent-based applications that employ multiple agents distributed across the enterprise. These agents:

- reside locally to monitor key software and hardware subsystems of mission-critical applications
- operate continuously, independently, and in parallel
- monitor specific parameters against predefined thresholds, for
  - the application
  - all associated software subsystems
  - the operating system
  - all associated hardware
- provide exception-based reporting, either via a local element management system or on their own, to a central management platform integrated into the enterprise management platform

Applications management is especially critical for client/server applications with distributed databases. The ability to monitor and maintain local database servers and accurately share data across the enterprise are crucial to the effectiveness of these kinds of applications. Examples of these kinds of applications include information systems, large-scale medical and financial management applications, insurance applications, etc. Management functions that are crucial to the effective operation of such applications include database management, configuration control, and software distribution. A representative architecture for managing systems and applications as part of an overall management infrastructure is depicted in Figure 5.9.

Applications management involves instrumentation and monitoring of specific applications and their impact on network traffic profiles. Applications management traces end-to-end conversations and builds impact scenarios for application changes. It enables network managers to know who is on the network, what they are using the networking environment for, what applications they are running, and how network response times can be

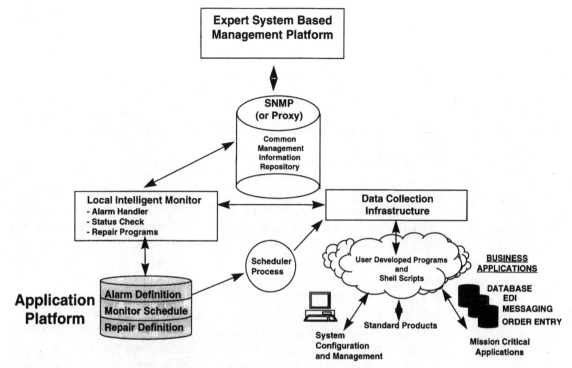

Figure 5.9 Systems and Applications Management Framework and Infrastructure

improved. True applications management tools are scarce. No operational standards exist yet, and currently available systems are usually proprietary.

Systems and Applications Management Summary

Applications management completes the management services environment by allowing it to manage all aspects of the enterprise. When the network, system, and applications management functions are tied into an expert system, the result is:

- faster identification of potential problems anywhere in the enterprise (i.e., prevention of problems)
- faster isolation, diagnosis, and resolution of problems throughout the enterprise
- truly proactive management across the enterprise
- the capability to provide complete service management across the enterprise

In addition to savings in time, staffing, and their associated costs, this approach yields significant increases in the overall capacity of the enterprise to support core business functions and achieve core business goals.

Issues in Managing Broadband Networks

It is no surprise that the current network management issues surrounding broadband in general and ATM (asynchronous transfer mode) in particular are only beginning to be addressed. Vendors and standards bodies are known for delaying work on network management until after a technology life cycle is well under way. With broadband technologies, this is a very serious issue. Broadband's very nature makes it uniquely difficult to troubleshoot and manage. Most of the general network management tools (e.g., protocol analyzers) and third-party SNMP platforms cannot merely be extended to manage broadband networks; instead, considerable investment is required to redesign them properly to support such technologies. For example, existing autodiscovery and mapping routines do not properly display switched internet configurations, nor do today's simulation and design tools provide guidance on such questions as when to use switched ethernet versus shared fast ethernet. With so many unmet management needs in existing mainstream technologies, most network management vendors will defer investments to handle what is still an emerging market.

As a result, integrated management will not achieve its nirvana until broadband becomes more mature; users will be stuck with vendor-specific element managers for the near future. This means, among other things, that end-users really should evaluate broadband equipment vendors on the quality and depth of their element management. Further complexities are created by the fact that many network managers will have to endure a transition period during which their networks will be hybrid—part narrowband shared LAN internet architecture and part broadband switched internet architecture. Because of differing ATM architectures (internal) from different vendors, it is unlikely that the generic router management provided by current SNMP managers could be replicated in ATM switches. Dropped cells will be the curse of an ATM network, since a single dropped cell means that an entire frame, which can comprise many cells, will have to be retransmitted. Analyzing performance problems—e.g., troubleshooting a problem with too many dropped cells—will require a detailed understanding of the switch structure, as well as the workings of the vendor's approach to congestion control. Managing the complex configuration data describing the setup of the ports on an ATM switch will be a major challenge.

Management Service Integration

As discussed previously in this chapter, a very important phase in the management of an information network (or of any network for that matter) is defining the operations environment. A key issue is integration of management services. This integration is the act of building interfaces between frameworks that include a shared data model, a common user interface, a compatible toolset, and/or real time data and information feeds. While organizations prefer best-of-breed applications from one vendor, the reality is that vendors have different areas of functional and technological expertise. So rather than implement a suboptimal single- vendor solution for the sake of standardization, users are often enticed to integrate best-of-breed functionality from multiple vendors. Most organizations have more than one network management framework, and each accomplishes only part of the required functions. Integration ties the frameworks from different vendors together in an attempt to provide a single point of information for network management.

Managing Distributed Computing Assets

IT asset management is defined as a systematic approach to managing IT assets, including information systems (IS) department staff, end-users spending time on IT support rather than focusing on their objectives, technology procurement teams, suppliers, facilities, hardware, and software. Effective IT asset management optimizes the use and deployment of those assets, using a total cost of ownership (TCO) approach when making investment decisions. Some key benefits of an enterprise asset management system are that it helps organizations to:

- optimize the utilization of all assets

- lower operating costs

- enable effective risk management

- enable business managers to see the entire inventory and learn how to fund it so as to achieve the best return on their investments

- unlock the promise of client/server computing, making business end-users more productive and decisive

- help IT managers to streamline licensing and manage migration, warranty, and maintenance for closer cost control

Asset Management—Problem Analysis

The tasks of controlling costs and maximizing return on technology investments have become more difficult in the current distributed computing environment. Technology assets are now widely dispersed throughout the enterprise, making them less visible and harder to track. Organizations without an effective enterprise asset management system are at a competitive disadvantage because they are likely to spend more time and money purchasing, upgrading, servicing, and disposing of their technology equipment and resources. A comprehensive enterprise-wide integrated asset management system is needed to enable organizations to see what they have, who is using it, how it is configured, and what the purchase price and current value of such information technology assets are.

The asset management discipline is undergoing a profound transformation and gaining heightened visibility in organizations. Increasing LOB and department authority over IT budgets and the resulting need to scrutinize and manage distributed IT costs have contributed to this trend. Most important, however, is the change in the nature of the costs associated with the typical IT asset. Traditionally, hardware dominated the capital component of the IT budget. This meant the IT asset portfolio could be viewed as a portfolio of "stocks" characterized by significant upfront spending, supplemented by a predictable stream of maintenance charges, and amortized according to established depreciation schedules. But today's environment is dominated by a variety of software (both licensed and proprietary), and service charges have outpaced hardware spending. Consequently, the typical IT asset will soon be best envisioned as a flow, characterized by a sequence of largely unpredictable cost events.

The tools that are available in the marketplace are essentially passive repositories for asset data. Although central to many IT business processes, they suffer from an almost exclusive focus on hardware assets, predictable cost streams, and the assumption that central IT organizations are the sole corporate agents actively incurring IT costs. New systems have emerged, however, that are conversely characterized by a focus on licensed software, auto discovery, and a recognition that IT asset costs are likely to be highly variable over the course of the asset's life cycle. Asset management should take on many of the characteristics of financial portfolio management, with individual IT assets being treated as more or less swappable, risky steams of future costs and benefits.

Asset Management—Strategies

Several organizations are placing asset management in the forefront of their IT strategies due to the chaos created by distributed computing and IT budgets going out of control. Until recently, organizations felt no pressing need to integrate either the data that describes assets or the business processes in place to manage them. The key to achieving efficiency in managing IT investments is to centralize data that describes the technical aspects of the asset, or that describes the conditions under which the asset was acquired, including its life cycle and financial details. The CMIR strategy described in earlier chapters should be the linchpin to realizing an enterprise-wide asset management system. A typical asset management process and a model are described in Figures 5.10 and 5.11.

Figure 5.10
Typical Process for Life-Cycle Management of IT Assets

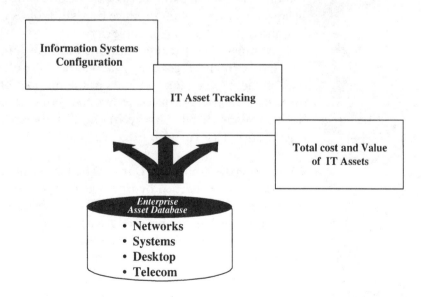

Figure 5.11
Integrated Asset Management Model

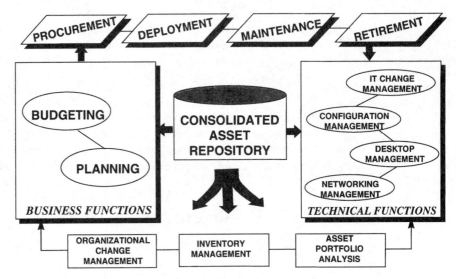

Some key drivers to a comprehensive enterprise asset management system are that: the productive lives of hardware and software products are much shorter than they used to be, and therefore purchasing cycles shorten and access to data that affects purchasing decisions becomes critical. Moves, adds, and changes to the IT infrastructure increase the complexity of the asset-tracking process, requiring either manual or automated tracking of assets. Current methods usually involve a manual tracking process through some home-grown methods. Large organizations have hundreds of product and service providers leasing contracts, and software license agreements often produce thousands of terms and conditions that cost money and increase complexity.

It is imperative that organizations establish business goals and strategies. Either financial goals (e.g., we will save $1 million by certain date) or data efficiency goals (e.g., we will cut the number of databases containing asset data in half) help to define the scope of the initiative. Then, a defined scope dictates where in the distributed IT infrastructure the organization first turns to meet the goals.

Characteristics of Asset Data. The first step requires a description of what data may be needed by multiple groups and, secondly, the method in which data will be collected to regularly update the CMIR. Physical asset data and the purchasing and procurement records are the two most critical stores of data to unite. Each contributes to reconciling a definitive inventory of deployed IT assets. In terms of implementation, integrated asset management systems should effectively populate the CMIR and should, likewise, have functionality to facilitate integration (e.g., data export, platform independence, and open development interfaces) with other asset-management-related technologies. The enterprise approach to integrated asset management eliminates duplication of both data and management processes.

Asset Management—Types of Data. With the proliferation of client/server technologies and the globalization of enterprise networking environments the blurring of distinctions between networks and systems is imminent. Clearly categorizing the inventories of an enterprise IT infrastructure becomes nontrivial and expensive but essential for establishing a long-lasting asset inventory database. There are literally thousands of data items that could be listed as important to any one user. However, there are four key types of asset management data (several data items can be grouped into these four categories) that are absolutely essential.

Physical Asset Data. This refers to barcoding or to serial numbers listed on each piece of major equipment not tracked by automated tools. Such equipment usually refers to legacy systems. This category of data is already tracked at least annually by most organizations. These are the only computing assets that pass through the traditional life cycle of physical assets. Many organizations still have computers on the same inventory reports as desks and file cabinets. While this approach may provide a link between computer and physical facilities, this traditional asset-tracking method does not significantly contribute to controlling dynamic distributed computing environments.

Physical Systems Data. Systems asset data include the personal computers and server systems' internal component parts such as CPU type, memory capacity, hard-disk size, etc. While too small to track from a barcoding or serial number perspective, system component data significantly affects what type of applications or network services may be available from a particular workstation or server. While this data has not traditionally been tracked on a dynamic basis, several tools are available to obtain the necessary data and deposit it in some predefined database. The challenge will be to reconcile this data with data obtained and deposited in the CMIR from other sources.

Network Connectivity Data. Knowing and managing the network equipment within the organization promotes efficient change management and growth planning. Currently, most network infrastructure equipment (e.g., routers, hubs, switches, and cables) data are captured through network management autodiscovery and physical device management tools. These data collected should be reconciliated with other data in the CMIR.

Application and Operating-System Software.   This type of data includes productivity office applications as well as development tools, database engines, database access tools, and system software, including the resident operating system. Integrating this software asset data with physical and hard-asset data gives decision makers a single source for strategic business planning.

An integrated database as described earlier should contain data from computers and computer components, network connectivity devices, and software license agreements. While data produced by discovery tools or network management tools may be available in a certain format, enterprise asset managers still have to integrate their own asset databases to relate that information with the business and financial aspects of the organization, making it a tedious and time-consuming process. Besides the problem of coping with diversified distributed applications, there is another set of challenges dictated by the necessity of having distributed, yet centrally controlled, operations related to asset management. Remote sites of almost any sizable organization need to work with centrally managed data and, at the same time, have the capability of leveraging a wide range of control over the data, depending on the authorization given by the central organization. The emerging internet-enabled intranet provides an excellent vehicle to deal with this problem.

Benefits of Asset Management

As more attention is focused on such areas as ROI from IT assets and increased productivity from new systems and software, successful organizations should formalize IT asset management strategies and policies. For most organizations, the benefits of deploying a single, enterprisewide IT asset management software system far outweigh the cost of implementing and maintaining the discrete procedures and tools.

Initial savings from enterprisewide IT asset management are derived from reconciling hardware maintenance charges and eliminating duplicate software costs. Gains will also be made by planning migration for hardware, software, and application training.

In a distributed organization, finance and IS groups must interact at multiple management layers to create an enterprise asset management program. These groups rarely communicate about asset management, except as a function of budgeting. An enterprise-wide integrated asset management has two important benefits: efficiency and effectiveness. Efficiency produces the longest useful life out of purchased or leased hardware and software and is resistant to change. Effectiveness recognizes that technology changes constantly and is concerned with adding business value by applying technology appropriately. The owners of these forces are the finance and IS groups within the centralized and distributed domains. Corporate business process reengineering, downsizing, proliferation in distributed systems, and advances in technology dictate that enterprises integrate both forces to produce a balanced and effective asset management program.

It is imperative that senior management of corporations make appropriate quantitative choices for every aspect of investment and return that affects the bottom line. The rules under which IT investments are made are changing to better reflect the creation of value through the utilization of information. While at times this value may be difficult to substantiate at the project level, it is ultimately reflected in the quality of the enterprise's decisions. These decisions, in turn, are directly related to the overall value of the organization—its economic value added (EVA), defined as after-tax profits less cost of capital—to its shareholders and principals. Further, the product as proposed will help companies in their activity based costing (ABC) and management. In the next few years, many IT organizations will use a customer-value pricing model to set chargeback rates. It is essential that these organizations have a good knowledge and visibility of their existing IT assets and their costs to arrive at these pricing models and to develop a value-based business model to make new capital investments.

SUMMARY

Managing globally distributed networking systems is complex and challenging. It is necessary to carefully plan its architecture and development to accommodate growth while providing increased network reliability. In addition, a real-time integrated management system with a common management information repository needs to keep pace with significant network events. The fastest such events are alarms, and the slowest are operator interventions and queries. All occur asynchronously and unpredictably. The system should be able to handle all types of situations, including an avalanche of events, such as those caused by a significant failure, without simply giving up and failing. It is extremely important to develop intermediate representation to handle such frequent events. Furthermore, it is imperative that the management system infrastructure be distributed to accommodate organizational distribution of personnel as well. To the extent possible, local filtering and automation should perform very temporal reasoning and try to resolve the problem condition locally before passing it to the central management site.

CHAPTER **6**

Issues in Managing
Internets and Intranets

Introduction

Internet applications are accelerating into a major force in the business world, and they are posing new challenges to network management in every organization. Some of these applications are designed for access over the internet, especially the World Wide Web, while others are based on corporate intranets that function on a web server/browser model. This chapter briefly discusses issues and strategies for managing the evolving internets, intranets, and other applications. Since the internet and its related technologies are changing faster than the speed of light, it is difficult for anyone to establish a management architecture that is expected to be stable for more than a few months. Hence readers are advised to refer to recent developments periodically and fine tune their overall management architecture to suit their changing requirements.

An internet is of limited long-term value if it cannot be managed properly; in addition, organizations could expend their valuable resources without any tangible business benefit. One can imagine the difficulty of trying to interconnect and communicate among different computers, routers, switches, applications, etc., if the conventions differ for managing alarms, performance indicators, traffic statistics, message logs, accounting statistics, and other vital elements.

Issues in Managing Internet Access

The internet's ability to reach millions of customers worldwide and its proven role as an efficient backbone for both internal and external communications has companies of all types and sizes scrambling to acquire internet access. At the same time, this access provides opportunities for abuse and misuse that can negatively impact productivity and expose the company to potential liabilities. A written corporate policy, coupled with employee education and the use of monitoring and management systems, can minimize these risks and encourage internet usage for legitimate business purposes. In addition, the internet backbone could be expanded to architect a more useful private internet—often termed an Intranet—a distributed collaborative workgroup application.

As companies expand their usage of the internet for such things as e-mail, electronic commerce, and collaborative computing, they are providing opportunities for their employees to be more productive. Access to the internet can help employees do their jobs better by providing them with a fast, inexpensive communication and research tool. Surveys of internet users indicate that as many as 80 percent of workers believe that the internet has improved their productivity. Unfortunately, internet access also provides opportunities for employees to waste huge amounts of time surfing the net, playing adventure games, and socializing with online chat groups. Many employees view the internet as a free service; after all, the company pays for the computer, the navigation software, and the internet connections.

It is nearly impossible for managers to detect most of the time spent in nonbusiness-related activity . For some employees, the allure of the World Wide Web is irresistible: the vast amount of information available for exploration—much of it in graphic form—and the feeling of being linked to a global community are too overpowering to ignore. The internet can be so engaging that hours may pass before the employee realizes that he or she has been goofing off and had better get back to work. Even with the best intentions, it is easy to get sidetracked by following all the links.

For the most part, access to nonbusiness sites on the internet cannot be blocked without resorting to firewalls, proxy servers, and other types of gateways that are generally expensive, complex to set up, and difficult to administer. Online abuse can also be detected with network-monitoring tools that measure network traffic. Organizations that use these tools are far less concerned with the content of the material employees access than with the time employees spend poring over it. They do not seek to protect their employees from the content but to ensure that their workers use the internet solely for business purposes during business hours. If traffic at a particular Internet protocol address increases at an unusual rate, the IS department can take a "snapshot" of whatever data the user is download-ing. The offending user can then be confronted with the incriminating evidence and asked to avoid online sites that have nothing to do with work.

A good internet access management tool controls employee use of the internet, including restricting access to unapproved resources. It allows a company to have multiple permission levels depending on an employee's job functions. Instead of unilaterally restricting access, the company can provide access to those who need it, when they need it. This type of tool can also report on use of the network and the internet by users and groups to facilitate department billing and the deployment of computing resources.

However, one should be accommodating, for a situation that appears to be idle net surfing may sometimes be an attempt by an honest employee to get familiar with the locations of various servers and to learn how to best navigate them. If this familiarization time requires just one hour per employee per day, a company can multiply the total payroll amount of employees with internet access by one eighth and add the cost of provid-ing that many hours of internet access to determine the true negative financial impact.

For some organizations, the use of internet access management tools may be the deciding factor in convincing them to provide internet access to all employees. Of course, the question that inevitably arises is: Who decides what are acceptable business resources and for whom? Vendors of internet access management tools generally provide, with their products, a list of sites that companies may want to block. Organizations can restrict or allow additional sites depending on their own policies.

The internet's ability to reach millions of customers worldwide and its proven role as an efficient backbone for both internal and external com-munications has companies of all types and sizes scrambling to acquire internet access and build business applications on top of it. At the same time, this access provides opportunities for abuse and misuse that can negatively impact productivity and expose the company to potential liabilities. A written corporate policy, coupled with employee education and the use of monitoring tools, can minimize these risks and encourage internet usage for legitimate business purposes.

Managing Internet-Centric Databases

The next generation of internet business applications will put access to the corporate database in the hands of web users. Already, the major DBMS vendors are releasing the tools for doing so. This section describes how controlling user access to sensitive data, maintaining data integrity, providing security, and making it all work over the World Wide Web are the next generation of challenges for both the network manager and the database administrator.

In the next year or two, all of the major database vendors will offer web-based front ends to their database products so that World Wide Web applications can be written to access corporate data in both internet and private intranet environments. As network management responsibilities merge with application management, this new wrinkle poses an extra challenge for organizations. Organizations are already facing significant challenges in managing distributed systems generated by client/server evolution, compounded by the internet and intranet evolution. Hence, as discussed in previous chapters, a technology-proof management architecture is a necessity and this architecture should be driven by a management information-based data model.

New tools for tracking and analyzing internet traffic will enable network managers to handle the outside internet connection with the same surety and efficiency with which private WAN connections are handled today. But the real push is not to give end-users the ability to surf the web—in fact, in many cases this can be counterproductive. The real push is to get business applications on the web server for a user community that may consist of the company's employees, outside customers, suppliers, vendors, and partners.

The pivotal element in this more pressing goal is the corporate database, which forms the basis of current business applications but is probably not ready for access over the web. And even if it were, the security risk involved in opening it to the outside world is substantial and could significantly threaten the very existence of the organization itself. Vendors are developing tools to mitigate these issues, as corporate intranets—private networks based on web servers and browsers as the universal client/server interface—are proliferating at a remarkable rate. Intranets have been described as a simple, industry-standard alternative to private groupware environments.

To position themselves for this growth market, the major database vendors are all lining up web enhancements for their products, and some are even delivering commercial versions now. These products will enable companies to create access to corporate data through web browsers while ensuring security, data integrity, and high availability.

Because of the unique characteristics of the internet/intranet-enabled network, the database administrator and the network manager will be called upon to work very closely together to set up these new applications. Applications management will depend on the soundness of the network infrastructure, and the job of networking management will be driven by the capabilities of the new generation of database products.

Internet and Intranet: Where's the Convergence?

When it comes to supporting web-based applications, a lot of developers think of the internet and the corporate intranet as two versions of the same thing. With the private network, one has controlled local access to the database. It is easy to identify the number of end-users that are likely to access the database at any one time. The traditional licensing schemes of database software, which are based on numbers of concurrent users, fit in well with this model. Even an intranet lends itself to this kind of licensing. But in a pure internet environment, there is no efficient way of predicting how many users will access the database at any given time. In trying to control this, organizations go to extremes in denying access to certain users or establishing other types of restrictions.

Another difference is in the area of security. On the intranet, the threat of security violations is minimal and the usual security scheme of user authentication handled by the database is adequate. On the internet, however, it is nontrivial to authenticate users so easily. It requires supplemental management control and applications to deal with access to the database.

Maintaining data integrity in a distributed environment of any kind, let alone a web application, is not an easy technical challenge. Methods such as the two-phase commit and data replication have been developed to handle the problems of handling multiple accesses where usage patterns are unpredictable. The ideal distributed database application provides what is known as location transparency. That is, it should be as easy to access remote data as local data, and users should be completely unaware of the physical location of the data. The web, of course, is an excellent example of location transparency because users work with a single system image, surfing the globe with the same ease as accessing a local server.

Location transparency requires a data dictionary. This data dictionary is for system use, not for human use; it describes the data that resides at each location as well as the information that the network requires in order to access it. Communications protocols, networking protocols, access method, and other related information is maintained in the dictionary, so that the system can automatically, without user intervention, create and maintain a connection between the user and the target database. The user references the desired table or database with a human-oriented synonym; the data dictionary translates this synonym into the technical name of the table, database, server, and network pathname, and executes the connection

Deployment of the data dictionary is an interesting technical problem. Some distributed databases utilize a global dictionary that stores information about the entire database, with all of its locations, in one place. This approach offers a single point of administration and control and avoids the redundancy of a distributed dictionary; on the other hand, it creates a single point of failure. Hence a good balance between the two techniques must be employed. With a distributed data dictionary, each local site holds its own copy of the data dictionary. This dictionary can be customized so that it contains information only about the sites and data to which access rights have been granted. A distributed data dictionary eliminates the single point of failure problem of the global strategy, but adds complexity of administration, since all copies of the dictionary must be updated each time a change is made.

Out of the distributed dictionary model comes a very interesting solution model that is, essentially, a new form of database management that is based on scheduled replication and e-mail. Implemented by some vendors, this model of data distribution allows individual users and locations to receive highly customized replications of data from other sites on the network. This model is used in the web-based client/server environment. When a user issues a request for action (such as data retrieval or update) on a remote computer, the request is translated into a remote procedure call (RPC) that allows database-to-database communication to occur. The

RPC is stored in the database as a procedure. This allows the user to call the procedure by a local name; the procedure, in turn, invokes the proper connections for accessing the remote data, executing the request, and returning the results. Users operating under RPCs need not worry about the technical complexities to ensure the transaction occurs correctly. However, management software applications must ensure that all code matches on both the client and the server. The database procedure must ensure that a transaction is recorded in its entirety or not at all. From a technical point of view, two key methods for accomplishing this are the two-phase commit and data replication.

The two-phase commit is used to guarantee transaction integrity in real time. The process entails two basic phases. The first phase involves checking servers to determine their receptivity to an update of their databases. The second phase entails updating the databases if, and only if, all the servers are ready. Two-phase commit is necessary when updates must occur in real time—that is, when changes to the data must be reflected instantaneously at all locations. However, because of its heavy resource consumption, this technique should be used sparingly. Another technique, called data replication, reduces the complexity of the application and also, for web applications, introduces an element of security into what might otherwise be a weak spot in the armor against hackers.

Security and Replication

Without a doubt, when it comes to writing applications calling for high security—for example, exchanging financial information such as credit card numbers over the internet—software developers are in a particularly vulnerable spot. An interesting architectural scheme that provides an excellent real-world compromise between interactive database updating and corporate database security is known as replication. This scheme is described in Figure 6.1.

Using this scheme, the corporate database (inside the firewall) is replicated onto a database on the web server (outside the firewall) by means of a secure channel. Internet and/or intranet users make changes to the replicated database only, and the corporate database is updated on a regular basis. This is a good architecture for developing a real-time integrated management system driven by a CMIR.

An advantage of the replication scheme is that the two databases need not be based on the same vendor's software as long as they can replicate

Figure 6.1
Replication Scheme
Protects Corporate
Database from Inter-
net and/or Intranet
Traffic

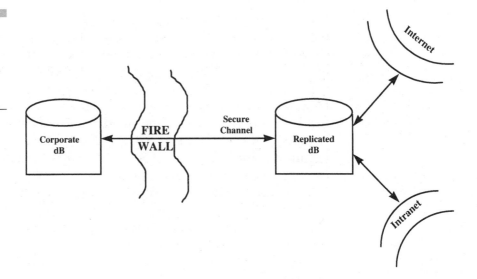

to one another. For example, a legacy DB2 database in the data center can replicate to an Oracle database on the web server, thus eliminating the need for application coding to support web server requests in mainframe DB2. Or, an Oracle legacy database can replicate to another Oracle database, simply to take advantage of the extra security of keeping the corporate data secure within the firewall. In addition, the two databases could be in different locations, thus enhancing disaster recovery as well. In either case, with updating on a regular basis—hourly, daily, or whatever works best—near real-time functionality can be achieved in an interactive management application without compromising corporate data security.

A variation on this theme would be to put an empty copy of the database on the internet service provider's web server and download this to the corporate database on a periodic basis.

Of course, saying that users can connect unlike database software sounds much more simple than it really is. When users employ a variety of systems, databases, networks, and query mechanisms, integrated data access can be quite complex. Industry-standard APIs are a good way to achieve heterogeneous access, enabling heterogeneous DBMSs and networks to interoperate. Gateway products provided by some DBMS vendors also enable heterogeneous DBMS interoperability. Finally, object-oriented technology enables one to solve many of these issues. Object-oriented solutions may appear as standalone products but are more likely to be incorporated into existing product categories. In fact, existing middleware products and transaction processing monitors are largely object based or object oriented already.

Lest we forget about the network manager, there are several important application management capabilities that DBMS products should provide, without which the management of the corporate database would be next to impossible. Among these are the ability to track ownership, revision history, and page modifications, as well as the ability to manage and synchronize content using transaction techniques and distributed database mechanisms. When looking into the new web-based add-ons to traditional DBMSs, one should ensure that such capabilities have been addressed.

Internet-Enabled Management Strategy

Chances are good that most organizations have some if not all of their network nodes hooked up to the internet. Now, some major vendors are talking about interactive internet applications that will change the way organizations do business. The internet, and now the enterprise intranet, will have to be managed effectively.

Today, managing distributed systems is a maturing discipline with clear pathways for the network manager to follow. One can purchase interrelated product suites, often from multiple vendors, that work together and usually solve management problems intelligently, rather than simply providing raw data that must be interpreted and acted on. Currently, the biggest challenge for managing data networks is not finding a product that can perform a task but working out a procedural paradigm that blends the capabilities of multiple products with the operations of the networking staff.

A new frontier is facing the corporate network, and it is sending those who have encountered it back to the management drawing board. This new element is the internet, potentially the greatest tool for achieving an organization's business objectives, as well as the greatest threat the network has yet encountered. This section describes examples of business applications that utilize the Internet, and outline the concerns that arise for the network manager when they become part of the internet and intranet operational environment.

Internet Applications

Internet applications are the babies being born every minute in today's software labs, and the armies of tomorrow's global economy. Although they are only now capturing the interest of IS managers and are fraught with complexities that have yet to be solved, they are real and potentially very powerful. These applications are being planned not only for operations on the global networked environment but for the corporate network as well, which will run like a private internet for the organizational user community. Standardization on the web server gives internal applications a universal user interface and a superior interface with the outside world through internet links. The internal environment, or intranet, works like a network operating system and GUI interface that is fully compliant with all internet networking standards. The feisty thing about internet and intranet applications is that they will soon be mission-critical in most businesses, and they know it. Major vendors are getting behind numerous development efforts, and previously unheard of startup companies are lining up products that could drastically influence an organization's future. In all likelihood, the corporate database will soon be the software foundation for custom internet and/or intranet applications that will reach an organization's biggest customer bases.

Unlike the traditional web pages, which tell about a company and its products, and perhaps provide a way to order goods via e-mail, fax, or phone, tomorrow's web site will be a totally interactive experience that ushers customers into the store, as it were, and handles the marketing, sales transaction, and all aspects of customer service in a single seamless application.

Some new-generation programming languages are being introduced to write "applets," web-enabled programs that run from a web server and use standard web browsers as the user interface. These languages are so important because their client interface is universal across just about every computing platform running today, whether the client is local (on the intranet) or remote (through the internet's World Wide Web). Another advantage of these programming languages is that it is a smaller, less taxing program compared to traditional programming languages. This feature is especially attractive for accessing applets via web browsers over the internet.

The concept behind internet applets that distinguishes it from the standard client/server application is that the web server is the new link between the client machine and the corporate database, as depicted in Figure 6.2. The client interacts with the applet running on the web server, and the applet accesses information in the enterprise database. All network links—between the client, the web server, and the central data repository—may be either LAN or remote (private WAN) or internet. This flexibility in the network configuration makes for the widest range of application versatility, but it also raises the most complex management and security issues.

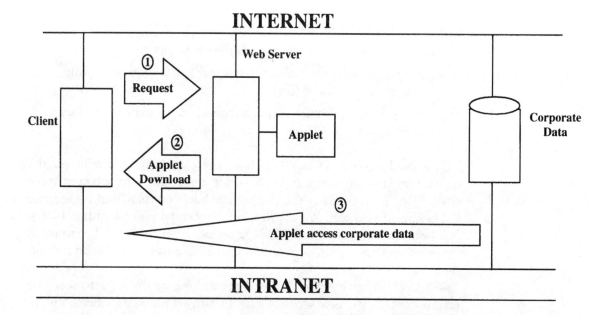

In an interactive Web application, the applet may be run on the Web server, or, with the advent of object request brokers, the applet may be downloaded to the client resource for direct queries on corporate data.

Figure 6.2 Interactive Web Application Model

Interfacing the LAN to the Net

The application environments made possible by applets such as those created using new-generation internet programming languages, as well as web servers and web-enabled corporate databases, are essential components of the total solution but do not address perhaps the most basic concern of all: How exactly does one safely and manageably implement internet access for the corporate data network? One of the lingering concerns with using a traditional LAN server as a web server is security. If one lets the outside world onto one's LAN/web server, one is essentially letting them into the private LAN.

Internet Security

Maintaining a secure internet environment is a subject worthy of volumes of publications; here we can only touch on how security figures into the general management picture. The manager of an organization's network has several main concerns when it comes to internet security:

■ securing the network from intruders

■ monitoring and controlling internal use of the net

■ securing the company's interactive internet applications, especially the electronic transfer of funds

■ providing high availability through redundancy and other business continuity methods.

It is hard enough to tackle each of these areas individually, yet the recent trends in intranets and groupware are making the job even more challenging by muddying the boundaries between them and upping the stakes across the board. Any application that can run on a standard browser, whether on the same local LAN segment or across the globe, inside or outside the organization, is potentially accessible and shareable on the corporate intranet.

Whatever specific form the internetworking environment takes, one certainty is that it is a security risk of unprecedented dimensions. To secure this wild frontier, strong measures are a must. An internet firewall is needed to protect the internal network from outside intruders. User ID authentication and encryption mechanisms are also crucial to the security effort.

In the foreseeable future, security on internet-enabled networks will look much like that on standard enterprise networks. Groupware applications will be shareable only within authorized user groups, and internet access, such as web browsing, will be centrally monitored if not restricted. Some internet services will not be made available at all, and others, such as e-mail, will use company-approved software. The organization's internet business applications will be isolated from the enterprise network by secure firewalls so that the outside world will have no way to gain unauthorized access. Network probes will routinely monitor for intruders and password guessing programs. Outside customers who wish to purchase goods via internet shopping will use secure electronic funds transfer methods as good as or better than those of any other sales media.

But how do we get there from here? For network managers who either consider themselves pioneers by nature or have been thrust into that role by their business-minded executives, there are a few products that are shaping the landscape now, providing a pathway to follow.

Firewall definitions vary, but generally the term describes a collection of devices such as routers, adaptive hubs, and filtering devices working in tandem and configured to ensure that only expressly permitted packets of data may enter or leave a private network. Approaches to meet this end differ, but, however it is managed, the firewall controls the choke point where incoming and outgoing internet service requests are permitted or denied.

Conventional wisdom calls for isolation of the web server from the corporate network. Firewalls are generally put on a machine separate from the web server because typical web server programs are simply too large and complex to be examined effectively for intrusion on the firewall machine. Setting up the firewall is only half the battle; then comes maintaining the security in an operational environment. It is essential to continuously monitor and probe the networked systems for any security violations. Hardware-based network monitors are great for monitoring internet-related traffic on LAN segments, but they will have difficulty in the new virtual LAN environment. Hardware probes need to be located on network segments and cannot probe beyond routers, which are fixtures on the internet.

Managing Intranets

Intranets, which use internet technologies as a suite to create integrated access to information for everyone in the enterprise, are the latest hope and the newest challenge for organizations responsible for managing and supporting the enterprise networking environment. The unprecedented growth in this new technology should be addressed with a fundamental process for change and service management in new ways. Solutions must handle scale, complexity, and decentralized change—and in an interorganizational, federated environment. A typical intranet environment is described in Figure 6.3.

The internet and the intranets need industrial-strength management that is secure and automated but whose level of administrative overhead does not overwhelm its advantages. Managing change in a secure manner will be crucial to maintaining the internet viability as service platform. WANs are getting burdened with interactive multimedia traffic. Today's uneven network performance and the serendipity approach to security may be acceptable in early experimental stages, but as businesses begin paying for internet services and as they being to deploy mission-critical applications over those networks and begin to base internal business processes on the availability of intranet access, lack of effective management capabilities will not be tolerated.

Some organizations are caught by surprise as their mission-critical systems become woven into the web, where distinctions blur between what

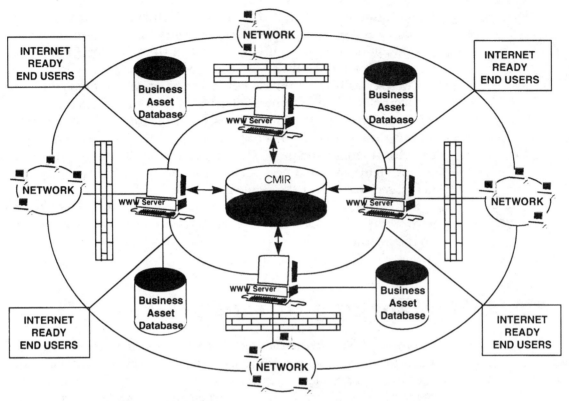

Figure 6.3   A Typical Intranet Environment

is "inside" and what is "outside." But enterprises are becoming more virtual and more porous, with lots of interconnections, including external links to suppliers, customers, and partners. As a result, the old approaches to security—setting up firewalls to control a network's perimeter—must give way to newer, more specific and finely grained security measures. These need to be applied at the resource level, such as granting access to a single database or file, or granting permission to use a particular application, and to be managed in a federated, decentralized manner. Ideally, it would be possible to enforce global management policies while still enabling decentralized administration of access controls and permissions.

The internet gateways get overwhelmed as new multimedia applications come up on the enterprise network without warning, thus making web performance enhancements a critical issue. Current web protocols require a large number of separate reads and writes between a browser and various servers to paint a page. This means that the response time on each low-level protocol request to a server is a key determinant of overall performance. To ensure good performance, servers should be within only a few router hops of the end-users using them. This dictates replicating server content to key regions or localities to keep round-trip times small. This strategy eases traffic loads on WAN backbones.

Due to the dynamic nature of web hosts, it is nontrivial to forecast usage of the internet or of the intranets. It will be necessary to discover how the intranet is growing and being used and applying that knowledge to automatically alter the location and distribution of frequently accessed web sites, as well as the mechanisms that invoke replication. Approaches to managing the web servers and internet services, such as name and security services, should be integrated with existing software systems. Specialized subsets of functionality will evolve at different rates to support electronic commerce, service delivery methods, global information access, etc. More emphasis is needed on managing applications that reside on the web and the supporting intranet infrastructure.

SUMMARY

Since no management product addresses every area, organizations must identify their biggest weaknesses, and use the product/solution that best addresses them. Of course there is more to managing internets/intranets than buying the right tools. Implementing effective internet/intranet management can mean persuading different parts of an organization to integrate management information. Managing internets/intranets is not easy but the consequences of not managing could be horrendous. The tools available may help one get started with the daunting task of getting a handle on the web and making a dent in operational efficiency.

Management systems for internets/intranets and the associated networking infrastructure must be open and easily integrated with the equipment from multiple suppliers. The management systems must enable decentralized change, and the information they discover about web usage and performance should be tracked and reported.

CHAPTER 7

On the Design of Global Service Centers

Introduction

The information systems challenges of global organizations involve analyses of how similar or linked activities are performed in different domains. Global information networked systems are employed to manage the exchange of information, goods, expertise, technology, and finances. Globally distributed systems allow the many business functions that play a role in coordination—logistics, order fulfillment, finance, and so forth—to share information about the activities within the organization's value chain. In global organizations this capability allows them to

- be flexible in responding to competitors in different countries and markets
- respond in one country (or region) to a change in another
- scan markets around the world
- transfer knowledge among business units in different countries (or domains)

- reduce operational costs
- enhance effectiveness
- preserve diversity in products and production locations

Although many global organizations have an explicit global business strategy, few have a corresponding strategy for managing their enterprise networked systems globally. Many organizations have information interchange protocols across their multinational organizational structures, but few have global networking service architectures. A global networked system strategy is a necessary response to industry globalization and national competitive posture. Figure 7.1 presents various alternative strategies to networked systems management (NSM) options that result from the evolution of the global business environment and technology.

A networked systems management architecture defines where applications are executed and databases are located and identifies the communications links needed among locations. The architecture is important for providing standards for interconnecting very different systems instead of enforcing communality among systems. This chapter will address some

Figure 7.1   Alternative Strategies for Global Networking Management

Business Structure	Coordination/ Control Strategy	Coordination/ Control Mechanism	NSM Strategy
Multinational/ Decentralized Federation	Socialization	Hierarchies: managerial decisions determine the flow of materials and services	Decentralization: stand-alone databases and processes
Global/Centralized	Centralization		Centralization: centralized databases and processes
			Linked databases and processes
International and Interorgani- zational/ Coordinated Federation Transnational/ Integrated Network	Formalization Co-opting	Markets: market forces determine the flow of material and services	Integrated architecture: shared databases and processes

Figure 7.2
Overall Organization-
al Approach to Man-
aging Global Net-
worked Systems

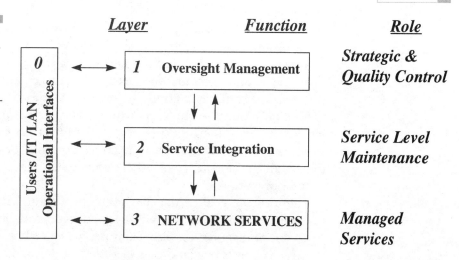

Figure 7.2
Overall Organizational Approach to Managing Global Networked Systems

issues related to distributed systems and suggest an architectural solution for managing a diverse networking services environment.

The use of standards and standard operating procedures is an important strategic policy, as many organizations today limit the number of inter-company formats they support. Given the success in developing and adopting global standards, procedures, and practices in specific narrow areas, one might argue that it is becoming more difficult to make "standards mistakes" than was the case several years ago. However, decisions about the components of networked systems and supporting management systems involve a move towards centralized, corporate management coordination and control, whereas decisions regarding traffic volume, data store, and service functions require decentralized planning and conformity to domain standards and requirements.

Management information data architecture defines the arrangement of management and control information within an organization. Although every organization that maintains data has a data architecture, in most organizations this architecture is more the result of the evolution of applications databases in various departments than of a well-planned common management information data management strategy. The overall functional approach to managing the global networked system is described in Figure 7.2.

Enterprise Service Center

The basic idea behind managing any globally distributed networked system is information movement and management. To that extent it is essential to define an enterprise service center (ESC) that will be the hub of all major activities related to service delivery and management of the entire enterprise, including both networking components and end-users. The service center provides the means for management of information so that relevant, sufficient, accurate, and timely information will be delivered upon request to the users who are connected to the network. The service center will have an operational impact on end-to-end services, information provided to local, regional, national, or international customers, and performance of other systems that require data or information for operation.

The ultimate goal of the ESC solution presented in this chapter is to maximize end-user productivity by focusing on applications as the starting point to diagnose problems and performance bottlenecks and to substantiate cost recovery and/or service level agreements for business managers. The ESC approach will enable the organization to determine what applications are consuming which resources at what point in time, how business end-users are to be billed, why a networked application is performing poorly, and what remedial actions need to be taken or have already been taken. The design goal for the ESC solution is to provide *proactive* management of the organization's network computing infrastructure.

Development of an enterprise service center is an iterative process that requires integration of the separate help desks, network control centers, and other support organizations. It involves a shift from a task-oriented, reactive mode to a process- and procedure-oriented operations mode. Critical success factors include, but are not limited to

1. defining specific end-user requirements, which, in turn, define the functional service center requirements

2. defining the consolidated service center mission, which documents the scope of responsibilities accepted and embraced by the service center personnel

3. defining the consolidated service center services, including the specific technologies supported by the service center, the method in which problems are resolved, and the commitment to support the service-level agreements developed by the consolidated service center for its end-users

4. establishing a single point of contact for all user services

5. establishing multiple levels of customer support

6. developing core processes and procedures, such as service-level agreements and chargeback

7. cross-training the service center staff

8. evaluating, acquiring, and integrating third-party management applications on top of the strategic management infrastructure architecture

Managing the Distributed Systems Environment

The focus of network management is the "care and feeding" of the network; the core task is finding a fault and fixing it; that is real-time fault and problem management. The focus of systems management is managing one expensive resource (typically a mainframe in the data center) shared by many users; the core tasks are administrative (i.e., change, storage, and scheduling management). The focus of ESC is the end-user; it addresses the management of multiple (global and local) resources shared by many users. ESC has its foundation in the union of network and systems management, but also embraces database and application management. ESC should include solutions for daily monitoring, administration, operation, strategic resource management, and capacity planning as well as for technology infusion, engineering enhancements, system integration, and other functional requirements. The development of an enterprise service center follows the methodology described in Figure 7.3.

Enterprise Service Management, as its name implies, is a service management framework, enabling more efficient and economical delivery of IT services in a distributed environment. The ESC should be driven by SLAs, a customer defined service for which the service delivery organization has committed a quantifiable and therefore measurable level of performance (e.g., LAN availability or maintenance response and repair times). The tools used to support the service delivery process not only provide capabilities to perform the technical work, but also the ability to capture performance metrics and monitor performance against established service levels.

Under the concept of ESC, the networked systems environment is treated as a utility, just as telephone service or energy are utilities. ESC encompasses the entire IT life cycle from requirements analysis through ongoing systems operation and maintenance. The central point of focus for the delivery of performance-based services is the ESC. As shown in Figure 7.4, the ESC integrates both user support services and networked systems management services. The help desk provides the interface to the network user while the network control function provides the interface to the IT.

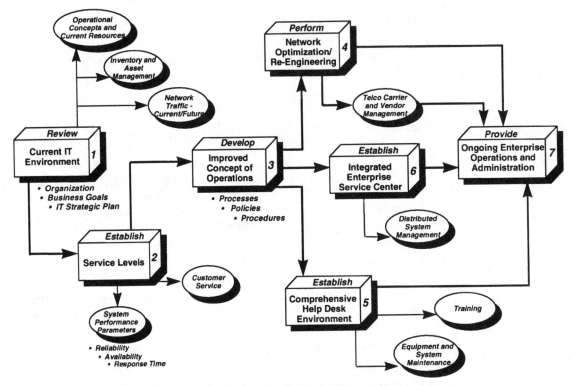

Figure 7.3 An approach to the Development of an Enterprise Service Center

These two elements work together as one unit, responding to service requests and problems reports to ensure that the network and associated systems are available and functioning at optimum levels. Figure 7.5 illustrates how an ESC could be segmented into domains and LOB units.

The help desk serves as the central point of contact to all users for all services provided under the ESC concept. Figure 7.6 illustrates how integral the help desk is to the delivery of networking services and for interacting with the end-user for optimum performance. In addition to providing a central point of contact, the ESC help desk provides end-to-end management of all problems and service requests. This means that as problems or service requests are moved to their appropriate point within the ESC structure for resolution, the help desk analyst who received the call continues to track it. This end-to-end ownership ensures that no service request goes unnoticed and that each is moved to resolution in accordance with the established service level or performance metric.

The ESC is also the centralized location for the automated tools that are used to monitor, manage, and operate the network. The ESC integrates

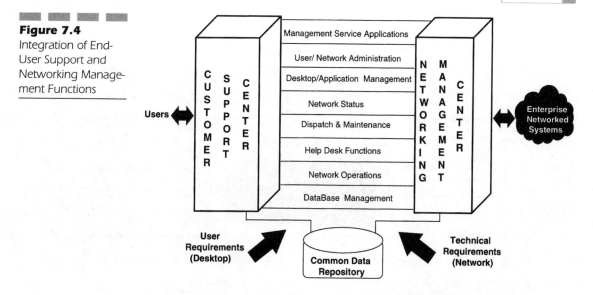

Figure 7.4
Integration of End-User Support and Networking Management Functions

tools designed to perform a variety of network systems functions through expert systems that provide two key capabilities:

Figure 7.5 Enterprise Service Center Based on Domains and Business Model

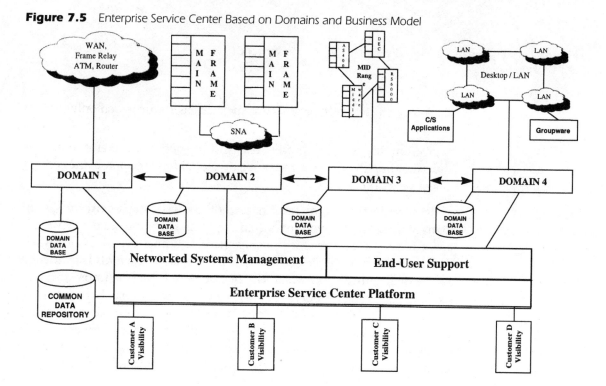

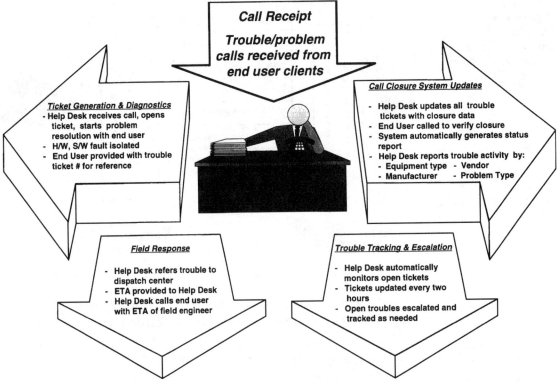

Figure 7.6 Establishing an End-User Support Service for Network and Desktop Services

- filtering of networking problems such that alerts are issued only for "real" problems

- problem diagnosis capabilities that assist the network operator in understanding the cause of the problem and taking the appropriate corrective action

Because of the fragmented nature of the industry's existing system management and network management tools, users and vendors have historically focused on reactive management: if something does not work, then take the appropriate action. By the late 1980s these tools had reached a level of sophistication where the degree of service was impressive and stable and automated operations were becoming feasible. Reactive management taken to its ultimate level of evolution (automated operations) espouses checking the various pieces of the infrastructure at regular intervals to see if something is broken and, if it is, automatically triggering a routine to fix it. In an environment with few sources (hosts), many users and relatively fixed connectivity (i.e., relatively finite and static points and causes of failure), it is feasible to write a rule or program for everything that can go wrong.

In globally distributed networked computing environments containing tens of thousands of elements, where every workstation can handle multiple applications and connectivity sessions inside and outside the corporation, the reactive model breaks down. Monitoring the individual elements of the connectivity chain between end-user and application without regard to the overall networked system and its dependencies, bottlenecks, and break points yields an overwhelming amount of data and no information. Also, it is not feasible to write a rule for everything that can go wrong in a distributed environment: the environment is just too dynamic and there are too many individual elements and conditions of failure.

A Typical Enterprise Service Center

Intelligent and integrated management of distributed networked systems poses several challenges: the collection and homogenization of management information from diverse network elements and distributed networked systems service components, the application of local and network-wide intelligence for correlating network events and isolating problems, and the ability to create a flexible and scalable management architecture that reflects growing and changing needs. Furthermore, the management information should be carefully identified and characterized such that it does not overload the network resources.

Intelligent management systems need large amounts of knowledge to analyze, operate, and diagnose the networked systems. These systems will provide network reliability and the ability to diagnose and resolve problems more expeditiously. Fault diagnosis, problem isolation, network topology configuration, and problem resolution are excellent candidates for expert system application and automation.

Intelligent management systems for managing widely distributed networked systems can become complex and the key is to keep it simple to attain the end objective of resolving network problems before the end-users notice any degradation in the service. In addition, the reliability, availability, and serviceability aspects of the network, while providing a mechanism for a CMIR for all the network configuration and management data, need to be carefully designed. The system should have the capability to analyze the networking problems to determine the cause, and then initiate appropriate corrective action (human or automatic).

The intelligent management system discussed here addresses two primary functions: network status monitoring and selection of appropriate control actions. Status monitoring involves the collection, consolidation, and correlation of network status events received from the managed network, and the detection and display of anomalies. Selection of control actions is usually based on a combination of heuristic, preconfigured corrective procedures, and explicit procedural algorithms. This is accomplished by a combination of distributed and intelligent application managers and use of formal commercial off-the-shelf rule-based expert systems. However, the architecture and design are flexible and scalable to accommodate any modifications and enhancements to the intelligent management system.

This section describes the key components that make up the integrated management system: the proxy engine (or local standard agents residing in managed components), management server, expert system, and management service applications. In addition, it describes the MIB and implementation details of the various components. The initial design of the alarm database is driven by the events that are typically generated by the various existing distributed networked components and mapping them to broad classes of *network* and *service* objects using a SNMP proxy engine. This is also applicable to real SNMP agents that reside in the components that support them.

The focus of this section is on an implementation approach of the necessary infrastructure for realizing an intelligent and integrated management system. Key management service requirements for managing distributed networked systems were discussed in the previous chapters and should be a straightforward development effort once the overall management framework and infrastructure are implemented. The event (and eventually, fault) management application will be a natural fallout of this discussion, as this is closely tied to the basic infrastructure. This is because the basic paradigm for managing a distributed networked system environment should be *management by exception*, which means that most of the management applications are driven by *events.*

Proxy Engine

The proxy engine (or protocol converter) interfaces the integrated management system with the various distributed networked system components either directly or through an element management system (all of the discussions in this section are also applicable to a framework that consists of regular SNMP agents as well as a combination thereof). These systems and components are assumed to provide only proprietary external interfaces, and the task of the proxy engine is to convert those proprietary management information to a standard management information structure. The standard network management protocol chosen for describing an implementation approach is the internet's SNMP. The proxy engine will support CMIP as applications and network elements become widely available.

Thus the main task of the proxy engine is to convert the management information in proprietary formats to the standard SNMP protocol supported by the integrated management system server. In addition, a novel approach to using a proxy agent is to enhance its capabilities to perform certain preprocessing of alarms and events, while acting as a gateway into the network itself. The two primary paths of data exchange between the element management system and messaging network components are the proxy engine and the management server. This arrangement is depicted in Figure 7.7.

One path reflects the processing of unsolicited asynchronous events (alarms) that come either directly from messaging network components or from their element management system. The other path reflects the exchange of information upon request from either the management server or the expert system to the proxy engine and ultimately to the network component. The information exchanged can be of two types: queries of

Figure 7.7

Proxy Engine and the
Management
Platform

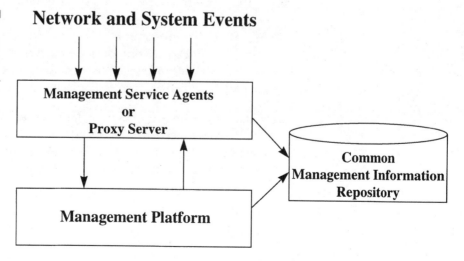

Network and System Events

configuration and status data, and requests for changes to the operational parameters to the network component.

The proxy engine's event processor collects the alarms from the distributed networked system components or their element management systems. The actual proxy engine itself is realized and implemented using one of several off-the-shelf products. Specifically, the proxy engine will have three different types of event handler: a systems event handler, a network event handler, and an applications event handler. A precursor to the development of the proxy engine is to identify and document all the events that are generated by different networked systems components along with their filtering, thresholding, and corrective action criteria. This significantly enhances the development of event handlers for different classes of equipment and the enterprise-specific management information repository.

The events are captured by any standard means that the element management systems are capable of supporting (e.g., fiber interface, UDP-based socket interface, or Async interface). Once the events are captured, each event is further analyzed and processed into an actual alarm, if necessary. Then the events and alarms are uniquely identified by event IDs. The processed events are then sent to the event processor.

The event processor, as described in Figure 7.8, receives the processed events from the various types of event handlers. The event processor updates the distributed networked systems management data repository with each arrival of event data. The event processor also implements the appropriate local filtering, event-to-alarm conversion, and thresholding as necessary. Finally, it converts the event and alarm format to the SNMP trap format and sends the traps to the expert system via the management server.

While the expert system server has the primary responsibility for consolidation, filtering, and correlation of network events, the proxy engine, as described earlier, provides intermediate capabilities to perform those tasks on a limited basis. The proxy engine should be able to do the following:

- Hold events that are identified as nonrelevant. The events are logged but do not become an alarm or an SNMP trap for the management server or the expert system. However, the information is stored in the repository for any future queries by the expert system or any of the management applications.

- Report events only if some other related event is reported from the same managed object within a certain period of time (short-term consolidation).

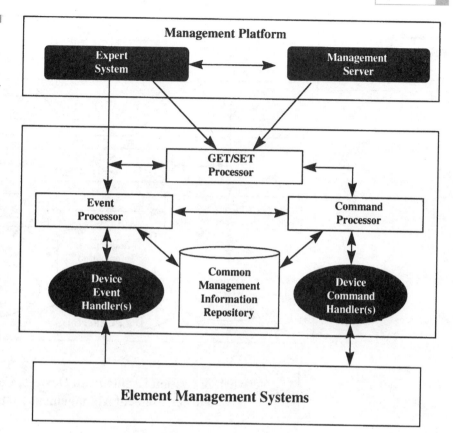

Figure 7.8
Event Processing in a
Management Service
Agent or Proxy Server

- Identify repetitive events and/or alarms and then generate *one* alarm or SNMP trap indicating that a certain number of alarms were received. This significantly reduces the number of repetitive alarms and nonproductive processing by the management server and the expert system.

The event processor described earlier should perform these functions.

Polling and Information Manager. The polling and information manager is responsible for issuing commands to the network components and element managers to get status and configuration information. This manager uses the commands native to the managed components and systems to retrieve the information necessary. The polling and information manager has two primary components. The first deals with the analysis of the incoming information and its appropriate structuring and storing in a CMIR. It is usually part of an off-the-shelf product and the actual interface is then added

Figure 7.9

Polling and Informa-
tion Management
Services

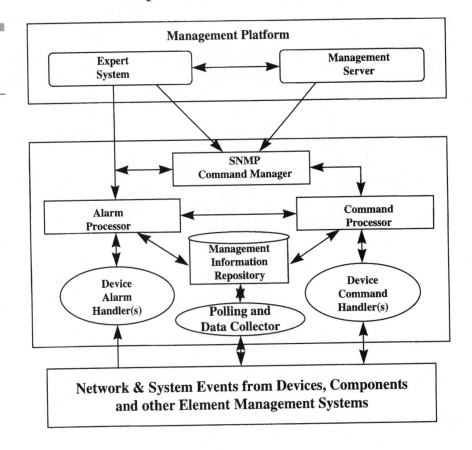

by customizing the polling and information manager. The second component is the actual interface to the network components and element management systems.

The polling and information manager provides instrumentation that
enables the management server and/or the expert system to start, stop,
and resume polling of the managed devices. This feature is intended to
avoid polling devices that are known to be out of service or have become
unmanageable for some reason. The polling and information manager
periodically polls the managed objects to keep a reliable and current state
of those objects. This caching approach is intended to avoid any SNMP
time-out problems that can arise when attempting to poll devices on
demand. In addition, this type of implementation significantly reduces
the management traffic overhead, while providing real-time status on the
state of the network. The polling and information manager is depicted in
Figure 7.9.

A key aspect of the design of the integrated management system is to minimize polling of the devices and manage by exception. Management by exception does not mean that the network operators wait until something goes wrong in the network, but rather provide instrumentation and local monitors (both reactive and proactive) to warn the operators sufficiently in advance of an actual component failing. This is easier said than done, but complying to this paradigm will ultimately result in a robust management system.

Distributed Networked System Component Controller. The component controller implements the interface to the actual components or the element management systems to modify their operational and/or functional status. When a request is received from the management server or the expert system, the component controller issues the proper command to the managed component to perform the requested operation.

If the management server or the expert system needs additional information, it has the option to directly interface with the managed component, thus bypassing the proxy engine. This option and flexibility are required and extremely important in case of a major failure in the network (e.g., a total node failure) creating an avalanche of events and alarms for the enterprise service center.

Processing a Request. The management server, the expert system, and all the management service applications should be able to send requests to the proxy engine. These requests are basically SNMP commands (Get, Get-Next, and Set) that manipulate the management information data repository.

The proxy engine uses the standard operatives to service the SNMP requests from either the management server or the expert system server. It decodes the SNMP command and issues the necessary calls to service the requests.

In the case of Gets or Get-Nexts, the information is assumed to be available immediately or not available at all. That is, Get and Get-Next commands will not result in native commands executed on the managed objects. This makes the polling and information manager responsible for caching the status information by doing periodic polling operations as discussed earlier.

For Set requests, the proxy engine decodes the SNMP command and issues the call to the device communicator for further processing. Thus Set requests result in actual native commands being issued to the managed object or an element management system. The device communicator is responsible for all these actions.

Management Server and Service Applications

The management server is the central component of the integrated management system for the distributed networked systems. It serves as the central communication mechanism for all management service applications and the expert system, and functions as a common user interface server for the end-users of the management system. As a communications vehicle, management server's role is defined in two modes of operation. First, it provides the means to propagate asynchronous network events to specific management applications that have registered to receive them in order to perform their intended functions. Second, it allows management applications to launch requests either to the proxy engine or directly to network components or to their element management systems to provide monitor and control capabilities. The primary mode of operation is depicted in Figure 7.10.

A typical sequence of events in the processing of a networked system event is described by the following steps.

Figure 7.10
Management Platform and Service Application Integration

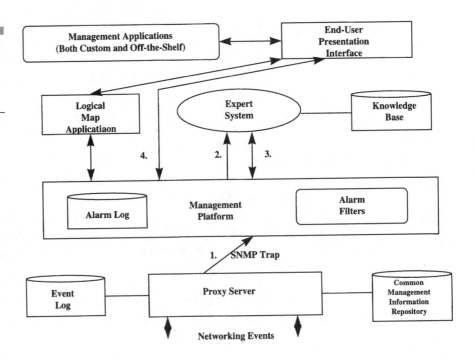

■ A network event comes into the system as an SNMP trap. This trap is either generated directly by a networking component or an element management system, or on their behalf by the proxy server. The management server will receive the event and compare it with the event configuration data (event sieves).

■ Based on the comparison with event sieves, the actual event (unsolicited) itself is forwarded to the expert system.

■ The expert system should then process the event and may initiate its own event in response, such as updating the status of a managed object either in the repository or on the graphical map that is presented to the network operator. Also, the expert system may seek additional information (in the form of a solicited event) via SNMP Gets or actively manage or update information via SNMP sets. This information resides in the MIB and can be accessed by the proxy engine, the expert system, or the management server.

■ Any event that updates the graphical view of the network (status event) can be forwarded to other management service applications requesting such notifications (this is accomplished by the management applications registering for those events).

One of the most important applications is operator (or end-user) notification of the status of the network, in real time. To that end, the application to manipulate the network map and its associated managed object is an important function of the management server. These map applications provide features such as event handling, placing managed objects out of service or in service, creating event sieves, alarm acknowledgment, and clearing of the alarm condition. There may be other map applications specific to a given network that could be easily added to the management server.

When a network event is received by the management server either from the proxy engine or directly from an element management system or a managed object, the event sieve manager performs the following tasks.

■ It forwards the event to any application, including the expert system, that has registered to receive these events.

■ If the event is local to the management server, it will forward it to the different event sieve managers of other servers (in case of a distributed management system) that have applications interested in the event. In addition, this task could also be used to update and/or synchronize any backup management servers for disaster recovery purposes.

- It will send a record of the event to the event log module for recording in the various event logs. In addition, it will add a unique identifier to each information unit in order to keep track of event sequences for diagnostic purposes. This identifier is extremely useful in correlation of alarms/events by the expert system.

To accommodate multiple alarms of different severity for the same managed object, the repository should be queried to see if an alarm of higher severity is outstanding for that element. Most of the network status is maintained in the repository. The events are also stored in the appropriate event log. The event log manager allows filtering of events that are stored or retrieved. Different logging criteria are also part of this functionality and can be viewed by any valid user of the management system.

The expert system will send status events to the network operators via the standard graphical user interface using the standard SNMP trap mechanism. This trap will contain the network component name and the new status. The user agent (responsible for updating the operator maps and windows) is capable of receiving these traps directly and updating the map, and is usually part of the management platform that is chosen. If necessary, this functionality could easily be developed using the management platform development tools.

When network events are processed by the management server and sent to the expert system in the form of an alarm (SNMP trap), or based on other event sieve criteria, the expert system may do one or all of the following:

- Issue an SNMP Get request to obtain additional data related to the event/alarm. This may be a query to the MIB, to the proxy engine, or to the managed object itself.

- Issue an SNMP Set request to adjust a managed object's configuration or operating state. If both Set and/or Get requires the services of the proxy engine, the expert system may take additional actions necessary to satisfy the Set and Get requests.

- Modify the map of an associated managed object within the operator's graphical user interface.

When a status change trap is received by the management server either from the expert system or from any other management application, the messaging services network map is updated. An operator is then required to acknowledge that it is working on a particular alarm by so indicating on the network map. This feature is implemented by doing an SNMP Get against the selected managed object to retrieve the list of outstanding alarms for that object. The alarm list can be displayed in a window and the operator can then acknowledge the alarm for that managed object. It is to be noted that acknowledging the alarm only indicates that an operator has taken ownership of the problem and does not indicate that the alarm is *cleared*.

When an alarm is received by the alarm acknowledgment module for a particular network component, an alarm acknowledgment timer will be initiated. Additional escalation procedures could be implemented here to ensure timely actions by the operators. The alarm acknowledgment timer will be started to wait for a user-defined or predetermined period of time. This is typically the normal period of time an operator will actually be working on a resolution of the problem condition. This provides a means for the network designers and engineers to document approximate recovery time for the various possible problems in the networked environment. These times should be analyzed, reviewed, and negotiated with the network operators and then become part of this alarm acknowledgment timers.

When this timer expires, a query will be made to the managed device that generated the alarm. If the device is functioning properly, the object will be returned to its normal state and the appropriate map symbols will be updated. In addition, the proxy engine will also be querying the managed object in question during this problem resolution period. If it determines that the object is functional and operating normally, it will send an SNMP trap to indicate that the status of the managed object is normal. In addition, the management information repository is also updated with the current status.

In some cases, either the proxy engine or the expert system may not be able to determine if the alarm condition for the managed object has been cleared. An override feature to interactively clear an alarm should be part of this module.

A feature to place a given managed object out of service or bring it back in service after it is functional should be part of the design. This includes such things as hardware replacement, network components under test, etc. The operators should be given the opportunity for specifying the time the managed device will be out of service. Most management platforms have a provision to place a managed object in the network map into an *unmanaged* state by a special color or shade. When this action is specified by the operator, the repository will be updated through an SNMP set to mark the action. The expert system or the proxy engine, as the case may be, will then stop polling that particular device for the specified time period, before the current status is sought. To bring a managed device back into service, the above procedure is reversed. The mechanism to toggle between managed and unmanaged state is an application that is developed using the management platform tools.

Expert System and Distributed Networked Systems. One of the biggest challenges in developing an expert system as part of an overall management platform for distributed networked systems is to identify a real-time system that provides means for automating small to large and complex tasks that are typical of such networks. Once this is done, it is important that a sophisticated interface be developed between the expert system and the management platform utilizing standard APIs and methods.

Development of a robust expert system from scratch can be a very time-consuming process and even wasteful. The development time is distributed among many functions, including knowledge engineering, expert system application development, operator interface development, data interface development, inference engine design, and maintenance and support. The functions and features that support the above can be divided into at least four classes: those that are specific to a given application (e.g., the model of a client/server application), those that are specific to a class of diagnostic problems (e.g., a knowledge representation of the failure modes of different network service types), those that are generic to diagnostic facilities (e.g., a bulletin board facility, an explanation facility), and those that are generic to all real-time expert systems (e.g., reasoning on time, alarm correlation, or bad value handling). Ideally, the development of a new application should only require the development of features that are either specific to the network service application or new generic features that have not been encountered before. Efficient development of real-time expert systems or, for that matter, any software, depends on the ability to reuse components that were developed earlier.

As with any software system that will be embedded into a real-time management and control system, there are several criteria for selecting an expert system shell: speed, interfaces to conventional languages for device driver support, flexibility, rapid application development environment, portability, the learning time needed to use the shell, product maturity, interface to leading management platforms, compliance with standard management and user interface protocols, and availability of third-party applications.

Expert System Driven Management Infrastructure. The expert system-management infrastructure interface is described in Figure 7.11. The expert

Figure 7.11
Expert System and
Management Platform Integration

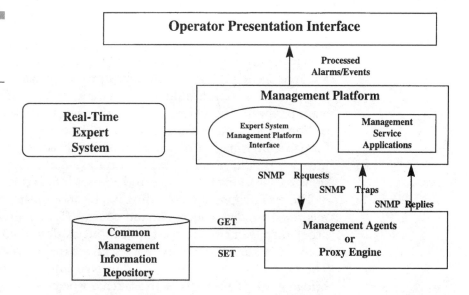

systems that are commercially available provide users a platform to write their own service applications. The actual interface itself could be a standalone application or embedded into the expert system applications. The interface specifies the connectivity between the expert system and the standard management platform using an API. The information could be related to transmission protocol or to API details of the management platform. The interface should also provide object definitions for specifying network configuration and topology information. The methods for sending exceptions and receiving exceptions, and the means for browsing and setting the management information parameter values of the network components are also part of the interface.

Real-Time Fault Management. The objective of real-time FM is to isolate and resolve problems that occur in the distributed networked system environment within a timeframe that allows continued and normal operation of the network. Economic incentives for real-time FM include network service availability, reliability, revenue protection, and serviceability of the network. The timeframe for real-time fault isolation and resolution for a distributed network usually varies depending on the type of network service and is assumed to be on the average of a few seconds to a couple of minutes. However, it should be noted that this temporal tolerance should be specific to a given type of service or problem condition to optimize system performance.

One of the key requirement for the management system to intelligently interpret data is that knowledge must be added to the system by a human domain expert. This knowledge should include models of management system behavior and interactions, and human experience and interpretations (heuristic). Collectively, this knowledge is referred to as a KB. Intelligent management systems provide greater network reliability and problem isolation and resolution than can be achieved with fault-tolerant hardware, safety interlocks, or other simple management systems. In addition, these intelligent systems should be designed so as to allow for human confirmation or override of conclusions and actions, and the interface should support creation of a log containing all system conclusions, explanations, and advice, and all user interactions and inputs.

The overall approach to adding intelligence to the integrated management system, data collection, and control flow is similar to developing other management service applications as described throughout this book. Events arrive to the expert system via the interface (bridge) module. The expert system can request additional information via the interface bridge. Events, summarized and filtered where possible, are communicated to the outside world or to other management service applications through the management platform and associated standard APIs. The expert system should monitor and filter events as they arrive. However, when an event arrives, it may be necessary to search the management information repository for additional information or current topology of the network. In addition, it may be necessary to poll network components and take corrective actions. The user interface to the operator or end-users of the management system should be the same as the overall management system user interface.

The expert system design for the integrated management of distributed networked systems is centered around the concept of being data driven. It should respond quickly and appropriately to changes in the process or network that it is monitoring. The approach to data acquisition and processing is similar to the overall management paradigm: interrupt driven and processing each new alarm as soon as it arrives. Most of the alarms that arrive at the expert system have been preprocessed either by the local device monitors or by their respective element management systems prior to its arrival.

Distributed Networked System Representation.   A good representation of the network is instrumental in the overall design of the integrated management platform. The representation will include both the logical view of the network as represented in the management server and the physical view of the network as represented by the configuration management application discussed earlier in the book. Additional information specific to the expert system is built up as needed. Because network services are best described in terms of the interactions of their component objects as described in earlier chapters, object-oriented analysis and development offers a convenient way to model the network.

Two central hierarchies form the basis of our object-oriented network model. The first hierarchy is one of network components in which are defined classes of devices in relation to superclasses of device types: nodal components (e.g., CPUs, trunk cards, or port cards), backbone devices (e.g., CSUs, DSUs, switches, routers, hubs, or terminal servers), transmission media (e.g., T1, frame relay, fiber, or wireless), data networking equipment (e.g., modems or front-end processors), systems and application components (e.g., message handler, message transport, or different types of network services). Instances of these device objects have a one-to-one correspondence with devices in the network. The second hierarchy is one of network topology in which are defined the more abstract components of the network: nodes, links, trunks, circuits, and other networking components. These can be thought of as structural or functional collections of device objects. Instances of these topological objects also correspond exactly to their real network counterparts.

The purpose of the inference engine in an integrated management system is to isolate a problem originally associated with a topological object to a single correctable component. During the diagnostic process, the networked system model is manipulated and updated as more information is gathered from the network concerning a specific problem. Two kinds of data are stored in the network model: network topology and configuration data and dynamic object state and status data. Quick access to a network configuration database is absolutely critical for real-time FM and hence an efficient database model of network configuration maps easily into an object-oriented methodology. When a problem is detected, relevant instances of topology and component objects are created through a series of predefined database queries. The database itself is automatically updated, either through polling for current device state and status or through event notifications from the management platform itself. On the other hand, dynamic status will be retrieved from the devices themselves. For certain state information the proxy engine or the SNMP agent will collect the information periodically and store it in the management information repository for any application to request such information. When the expert system requires state information on the network component, it should retrieve the necessary information either from the repository or directly from the device itself depending on the temporal tolerance for such information.

As discussed earlier, class design for an expert system includes definition of physical and logical objects and their attributes. This class design is similar to the management information development, and commonalities are established between the two functions. Class definition also includes recognizing commonalities to build abstract *superclass* in a hierarchy to take advantage of inheritance, which simplifies reasoning, problem isolation, and resolution. As the management applications mature, it will probably be desirable to continually make the expert system more sophisticated. To support enhanced capabilities it may be necessary to create new subclasses. While the subclasses are easy to add due to the flexibility of the expert system chosen, it may take sizable amount of time to go through all the instances of each object and rebuild them as instances of more detailed subclasses by making a decision about each object, its attributes, and its overall fit into the model of the target network. Careful thought should be given to the class *software processes* that is the core of any network.

The expert system structure is organized by *part-of* hierarchy, from software processes and low-level hardware, through higher-level hardware, transport segments, WANs, sites, etc. This is represented by subworkspaces of objects as is done in the management server, thus facilitating better communication between the two. This hierarchy is easy to modify as needed, since the subworkspaces include *containers.*

Expert System Class—Networked Systems. This is an important set of classes for the distributed networked applications. Attributes of the various service processing components include in/out of service indictor, test state, etc. The attributes also specify associated expert system operatives including the names of an abstracted *polling method,* such as ping or SNMP Get of the object name. Similarly a test method is also specified for each object class. A design goal is to optimize the number of attributes of the service processing components, software processes, etc., since there will be so many of them. This way the expert system's manager process can focus on certain key areas, and only needs to maintain information in areas of immediate interest based on recent events. An alternative would be keeping the state of every object in the object definition itself. Also, any diagnostic or correlation conclusions are properties of the expert system manager, not of the service processing components. Thus, multiple expert system managers using different diagnostic techniques should logically be set up to use the same approach.

Another attribute of service processing devices or software processes is the *time-last-proven-good.* This is used in diagnostic logic. If multiple expert system managers draw conclusions about an object behavior, they all get the benefit of any recent analysis or testing. Still another attribute is *test-state*. This is not just a property of a manager, since the device behaves differently when placed in test states such as a remote loop back mode, or restarted.

Expert System—Network Services Modules.   This major set of classes has several major subclasses. The network services modules that are managed and proxied as SNMP devices are treated similarly to the service processing devices. Other modules are specialized, such as the local network application managers and proxies themselves, and the objects associated with the different components of the integrated management system.

The expert system manager process is a subclass of software process. It has attributes needed for monitoring and control, such as specification of polling intervals, and a variety of lists used to record aspects of the structure and state of elements in the network. For instance there will be an *outstanding-polled-list,* which is a list of objects that have been polled but for which no response has been received yet. The *failed-poll-list* includes objects for which a poll has timed out, and will also include objects for which alarms have been received. The *suspect-list* is a list of devices that are not pollable, but could possibly be a cause of a problem. The *proven-good-list* is a list of devices that can be proven to be good, based on tests. For instance, a successful polling results in placement in the proven-good-list. Similarly, intermediate objects on a unique path to a successfully polled object are placed in the proven-good-list. The expert system manager also maintains a list of reachable and nonreachable devices, based on the network topology.

Expert System—Containers.   This class includes sites, node clusters, LANs, domains, etc. The expert system passes connectivity information from an object to its subworkspace, so that a hierarchical representation can be achieved. A connection made to a container object automatically generates a "connection post" on the subworkspace of the object. Objects connected to the container are also considered connected to objects on the subworkspace. For instance, an order entry application is a container. At a high level, domain X is connected to domain Y via order entry application. At a lower level, a specific transport gear or circuit may make the more detailed connections.

Expert System—Connections.   A class hierarchy is also developed for connections. For instance, a T1 link is a subclass of node link. From an implementation standpoint, it is better to build most of the information into objects for several reasons. When connections between objects are broken up by intermediate connection posts or junction blocks, each little connection segment is considered a separate connection. It then becomes necessary to propagate attribute information between these segments, possibly adding extra processing and analysis.

Several object types such as remote link are provided as normal objects rather than subclasses of connection, so that when the diagnosis needs to consider line failure, the diagnostics have an object to refer to.

Expert System—Events and Faults. The basic structure representing events and alarms is the expert system message with attributes. A subset of the attributes will map directly from those received via the management server (sending device, ID, time, etc.). There are additional attributes associated with the incoming events for fault management purposes. This includes the alarm acknowledgment status, ID of the operator who acknowledged the alarm, alarm clear time or status, etc.

It is expected that the attributes of the messages will include a revisit-method attribute, specifying a procedure when the revisit time is reached. This feature is used to support time-out on acknowledgment, time-outs on expected time to repair, etc. At any time, the revisit method and time can be changed so that an alarm message can go through a series of time states and state transitions specified by the revisit methods. There will also be a repetition-counter attribute for alarms. This will be used to filter alarm messages, so that only one copy is maintained for alarms corresponding to the sending object, target object, and message ID. The occupancy of multiple alarms for the same object is minimized by local monitors, element managers, or SNMP agents (or smart proxy engine) as discussed earlier.

Problem Isolation and Detection. An initial task in the diagnostic process is problem detection. Each problem must have a unique description in terms of an affected topological or network object and its failure mode. Problem detection involves a heuristic mapping of alarm patterns to problem conditions, which is usually best accomplished using forward chaining rules. As new alarms are read by the expert system manager, their specific attributes become facts in working memory. Along with affected component and failure mode, other problem attributes set at creation might include failure status, severity of the problem, and a list of associated alarms. A data abstraction model needs to be adopted for a given diagnostic approach. The creation of these problem abstractions allows a more generalized set of rules to map to possible causes.

The notion that a subset of indicators is necessary and sufficient to establish the existence of a problem is very important. Some alarms are consistent with a problem's existence, but are neither necessary nor sufficient in themselves. It is important to determine when intermittent problems clear themselves. In addition, some alarms may be inconsistent with the existence of a problem, indicating another problem condition instead (the device reporting an alarm may not be the problem device—sympathy alarms!). In managing distributed networked systems, it is important to recognize causal relationships between coexistent problems and implement the correct diagnostic strategy. In effect, the expert system should create all problem instances whose existence is supported by the incoming alarms, and use of the knowledge on causality to decide which problem to diagnose.

Diagnosing problem conditions in a distributed networked system environment starts with a set of observable symptoms (e.g., transaction traffic backing up or user services congestion), which are events coming in as warning messages and in certain cases as alarms from local monitors and element managers. The general processing scenario of incoming events is depicted in Figure 7.12 and follows this sequence:

- decoding of the alarms and events as needed
- filtering of events to eliminate obvious repetitions
- creation of ES messages and placement in the *symptoms* message handler
- selecting candidate *most-likely* failures based on a specific messaging services model or other information
- running additional automated queries and/or tests where possible
- model-based diagnosis, drawing conclusions about root causes and sympathy events when possible, proving network components *good* or *bad*
- clustering the remaining alarms into reasonable groups when possible
- notifying the operator or end-user with summarized alarms and mystery alarms, either directly or via the management server

A model-based approach in combination with clustering of events and alarms provides a powerful reasoning method. Incoming events and alarms are mapped against their corresponding objects in the expert system. If there is no associated specific object, a new one will be created and placed within a broad class's workspace hierarchy, based on predefined and established hierarchical naming conventions.

Figure 7.12
Event Processing Ser-
vices in an Expert Sys-
tem Management
Environment

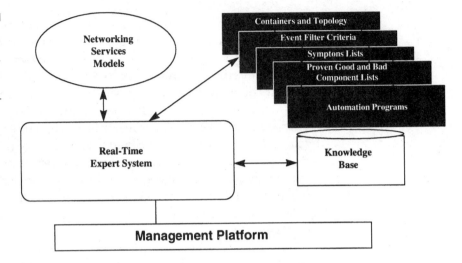

Figure 7.12
Event Processing Services in an Expert System Management Environment

By analyzing a pattern of events, it may be possible to choose one or more objects as the ones most likely to have been the actual initiating failure or the *root cause* for some cluster of events and alarms. In some cases, additional test procedures are conducted. These tests are identified by name in the test-method attribute of a device. Once new problem instances have been created, their relationship to other problem is established. Some problems cause multiple side effects whose appearance depends on circumstance and local topology. For example, when a node experiences an outage, all services, systems, and circuits going in and out will be down and all traffic passing through that node will be rerouted. In order to establish the relationship between problems at the specific service level, the expert system should recognize this node as their common nodal point consisting of building blocks essential for the operation of the network service. This is accomplished by referring to the topology of the node and thus allowing the use of rules that apply heuristic knowledge about specific known causal relationships. In addition to topological adjacency, temporal adjacency is required to establish links between root problems and their side effects.

As discussed earlier, one diagnostic approach is based on comparison of the distributed networked systems model and the observed events. The model could be structural, thereby based on reachability—based on connections, and in/out of service indication. It is also based on behavior specified in the object attributes. When these basic structural models are available, isolating a problem condition becomes less difficult. In particular, it is more likely that causality will be more obvious, so that sympathy alarms and root causes of problems may be more clearly separated. Also, distinguishing the most likely problems among a whole cluster of related alarms becomes simpler.

Clustering of symptoms means that the symptoms are grouped together based on some likelihood that they may be related. The purpose is to notify the operator with fewer alarms that provide a summary of hopefully related symptoms for them to further troubleshoot the component, if necessary. If all possible model-based diagnosis and additional queries into the device provide insufficient information, then the outstanding unresolved symptom will be clustered to the extent possible.

Clustering in the absence of models is a heuristic strategy, and one that may sometimes lead to wrong conclusions. Even when some symptoms are grouped incorrectly, this should not cause a problem for the operator. In the explanatory message sent to the operator, a summary of symptoms should be documented, so that no information is lost. The clustering of alarms can be thought of as grouping them into equivalence classes. Clustering alarms by timing may sometimes be effective when they do arrive, based on the same no-two-failures-at-about-the-same-time heuristic. However, a single device failure may cause events to arrive at drastically different times, for a variety of reasons. For instance, if there are no incoming and/or outgoing service requests to a specific order entry application that has quietly failed, no error messages may appear until a routine poll by a local monitor. Even in that case, they may not be confirming alarms from other service components that are dependent on the order entry application failed, since they are are not talking to it. A variety of alarms may still be *building up* towards their thresholds, which have not yet arrived. Thus, the absence of an alarm within a time window should not be used as positive evidence, unless some active queries are performed by the expert system manager.

If the additional queries and tests do not generate enough information after some time delay, the outstanding unresolved symptoms will be clustered to the extent possible, and summary messages will be sent to operator. *Mystery alarms* that cannot be clustered will also then be sent to the operator, all via the management server.

It may take some time for all alarms related to a particular network problem to arrive at the expert system. The more messages it receives, the more information it has with which to reason. Thus, there is an incentive to delay sending unresolved mystery alarms to the operator. Similarly, there is an incentive to delay sending messages about nodes that are suspect but not yet considered a likely failure.

On the other hand, the operator obviously wants to know about problems as soon as possible. Thus a balance needs to be struck on an acceptable time delay between the expert system receiving a message and some notification going out to the operator. A consistent approach should be established and is usually local to a given network operations and control environment. In some cases, it may be desirable to guide the operator through a series of tests, watching the results, and possibly logging the information. A mechanism for operators to close problems must be provided. In certain cases, clearing alarms as discussed previously will clear the associated management information repository entry, thereby notifying the expert system of the situation via an event notification.

Expert System Summary.   A true intelligent system imitates human reasoning: troubleshooting a real-world multivendor network often requires intuitive reasoning that an intelligent system cannot imitate. Systems are logical and incapable of making intuitive leaps to solve a problem. The expert systems available today for network management applications are limited by their support for multivendor networks and the capability to adequately blend declarative and procedural programming functions—blending *how-to* and *step-by-step* procedures in arriving at a conclusion.

Expert systems are strictly bound by the information contained in their databases and the procedures used to enter the initial examples. Expert systems can only come to conclusions or make recommendations structured within the logic of the rules entered into them. Quite often, additional testing and even slight changes in the rules or information result in vastly contradicting results. In addition, even the best knowledge engineers may not elicit complete and clearly verbalized rule sets from the experts. One of the key advantages of using an expert system for managing large globally distributed networks is the ability to compare several possible solutions and to help the human operator or manager arrive at a quick conclusion by eliminating several alternatives.

Expert systems should be used as part of an overall networked system management strategy and not just by itself. A management paradigm must be defined and established and a strategy developed for expert system-based management systems, and their capabilities and limitations must be understood. Primarily, intelligent management systems are diagnostic tools; they generate exhaustive data on network problems encountered in daily operations. It is essential that the management system designers customize, analyze, and use the data to eliminate common problems and ensure that the network performs to optimum efficiency. This is done by frequent interaction with the network managers and analysts.

Thus the immediate and long-term benefits of using intelligent management systems lie not so much in cost savings but in improving the network's performance and overall effectiveness. Over the long term, cost efficiencies can be realized in network operations and improved services in terms of decreased downtime, efficient and effective problem tracking, quick problem isolation, and, above all, proactive problem detection and recovery.

Features and Benefits of an Integrated Approach

There are several points of commonality among help desk, reporting, performance monitoring, network design, future technology, project management, fault management, problem management, configuration management, security, and migration. The following are the benefits of an integrated approach.

Better Performance. In a network environment with distributed resources, good performance depends upon all elements working in an integrated fashion. With multiple departments responsible for various parts of the network—the PCs, servers, applications, databases, LAN components, transport network, and mainframes—it is more difficult to tune the network properly. An end-to-end monitoring and management approach is absolutely essential from both a risk management and a performance perspective when a corporation migrates its strategic applications into a client/server environment or from a client/server environment to some other environment.

Lower Cost. The obvious benefit of an integrated approach is that it reduces the administrative overhead associated with manning multiple call desks, fielding multiple trouble tracking systems, supporting multiple program management structures, and so on. The capacity to perform true end-to-end capacity planning and optimization also allows increased efficiencies.

Consolidated Reporting and Trend Analysis. A consolidated report and analysis on all trouble calls from an enterprise-wide perspective provides a better picture of the overall health of the organization's networking infrastructure, and wider experience volume upon which to build a knowledge base.

SUMMARY

Managers of globally distributed networks are learning history the hard way—every time they try to get a fix on what's happening out on the networked system. Although they've got client-server technology that lets them run mission-critical applications across hundreds of sites, they are most often stuck with outdated and inflexible management platforms that are relics of the centralized past. What they need are client-server platforms that match the networks they're intended to oversee. That means fully distributed client-server management systems that use object-oriented common management information repository to share and process information across far-flung sites, not to mention a graphical user interface that runs apart from the other components of the platform.

Although these requirements are simple from a users perspective, network and systems management vendors have a long way to go— they've started redesigning their gear along client-server lines. In the meantime, organizations have little choice but to build a few components that are crucial to their management of the distributed networked environment. Irrespective of the vendors offerings in this area, user organizations will have to customize and tailor their management infrastructure to suit their needs. By using several available graphical user interface software, for example, they can set up multiple consoles and view information on the central platform. Another option is to localize SNMP polling and data collection, thereby saving bandwidth and reducing the processing requirements of the central platform. In this scenario, server-to-server communications, intelligent agents, or even a centralized "manager of managers" can be deployed.

None of these fixes qualifies as true distributed management, since they lack the client/server underpinnings that would allow servers and consoles to share processing and pass information to one another. But they are an improvement on centralized systems, most of which use SNMP to poll the status of remote devices (a technique that eats up bandwidth, especially on expensive WAN links) and take a performance dive when asked to control more than a few hundred devices at numerous locations.

Follow the Sun

One of the most economical ways to service a globally distributed networked system environment is by distributing the enterprise service center at strategic points. This enables the organizations to literally follow the sun in providing management services for the entire global organization. The economies of scale are attained in the usage of local talent and taking advantage of time zone differentials when planning for resources to staff the service centers. In addition, each of the service centers could act as a backup and a disaster recovery/business continuity site for continuous operability of the target networks.

The size and complexity of today's distributed networked systems puts a strain on the management infrastructure that most organizations use. Most available management platforms consist of a management server (which gathers management information from the entire network) and a console (on which the management information is viewed). The central console is usually the only place to view SNMP data—an impractical way to manage distributed environments, where managers in several globally distributed locations may need a console view at the same time. So some companies are opting for a cheap and easy way to spread the view of information across more remote sites without replicating management systems at every location.

True Distributed Management

Distributing management servers across the network sounds like a sound strategy, but what happens when these far-flung servers need to exchange information? Most platforms rely on internal databases for processing management information, and some type of messaging is required for sharing data across sites. In large networks where management platforms are proliferating, the need for server-to-server communications is a must, particularly because those platforms do not boast the technology that would permit real-time updates among servers. A reliable strategy is to distribute the common management information repository across the network, as discussed earlier in the book. Since most remote sites that are responsible for managing and maintaining their pieces of the distributed network require management information rather than pretty graphics, it would be better to distribute the management information rather than anything else.

Server-to-server communications has obvious advantages. Spreading the traffic among several servers takes the burden off a single platform, which might otherwise slow to a crawl—or even crash. The local management server can also perform SNMP polling, which reduces the amount of data crossing the wide area. Together with distributed data repository, this approach is also crucial to implementing follow-the-sun management, where control of a large network is shifted from site to site. For example, a company can use server-to-server communications to establish its central management platform in London during business hours there, and when the day is over shift it to New York.

Using local intelligent agents (custom or third-party provided) is another alternative. These software packages assume the role of the management server by polling local segments; they then sift alerts and contact the central console as an agent on behalf of local devices. These were discussed earlier in the book as part of the system and application management. Some intelligent agents are equipped with automation features that enable them to respond to local problems as they occur—by activating a trouble ticket, restarting a program, or swapping in a spare server, for instance. In addition, some packages work with a variety of protocols, filtering events from legacy platforms as well as SNMP devices. When used with other methods of distributed management, intelligent agents make hierarchical management of distributed networked systems possible. They act as go-betweens for local segments, while management system consoles serve as domain or regional site managers.

Putting It All Together

Multiple consoles and servers may help net managers distribute management tasks across far-flung client/server networks—but they all come up short in one key area: centralized control. That is why some organizations have chosen a manager-of-managers approach. In this scenario, a central system is set up to gather management data from multiple devices or management platforms at remote sites. LAN administrators handle the day-to-day tasks at the local sites, while the IS manager has a universal view of all information from all management systems. A manager of managers converts alarms from nearly any kind of system or device—including SNMP platforms—into a common data format that can be used to monitor and control events throughout the network.

Since this type of system does not poll the network but takes in alarms and alerts from other management platforms, the bandwidth penalty is reduced. Most manager-of-manager systems also feature alarm correlation and automation capabilities.

Using intelligent local agents with management platforms will enable organizations to better monitor and control all aspects of a particular network segment, including the systems on which mission-critical software is running. Many management functions (such as software upgrades, configuration of new users, and file backup) will take place automatically. Event reporting will be faster and more specific.

To provide such sophisticated capabilities, organizations will have to make radical changes to their management infrastructure. Consolidation and coordination of management databases will be one task. Today, most platforms use different databases for different types of management information. These databases must be not only consolidated within the individual management server at each site, but coordinated across multiple management servers in different locations. Using just one database per management server solves part of the problem but it does not address the issue of coordinating the database in one server with that in another. The CMIR approach described earlier in the book lends itself to this strategy. The solution is to merge each of these individual repositories into a single, object-oriented database—and then use an object request broker to keep data synchronized.

CHAPTER 8

Outsourcing Networked Systems Management: A Business Alternative

Introduction

Once considered an option for small or technically primitive organizations, outsourcing has become a realistic alternative for maintaining and managing complex distributed communications networks. Outsourcing services have diversified as the technologies they manage have grown in complexity and operational difficulty. The economic drivers are prompting many organizations to investigate outsourcing as a means to conduct their business more efficiently and effectively. Many network managers, especially those handling large, global networks, look to industry experts for assistance in managing their networks. Local and interexchange carriers as well as network management system vendors offer different outsourcing services, including facilities management, managed data networking services, or specific voice management services such as call accounting, cable management, and toll-free, private, and switched-line services management.

As a whole, outsourcing is rising dramatically in the economic priorities of organizations. Although different types of outsourcing have existed for years, outsourcing resurfaced recently as a plausible alternative to in-house data and voice networking and network management. Networking management falls into one of outsourcing's high growth areas since it constitutes a selective service that users can outsource without handing their entire IT department over to an outside vendor. Here user organizations farm out a dynamic operation like networking or a time-consuming and tedious procedure such as call accounting to a service provider. These contracts often last three to five years, as opposed to the long-term ten-year contracts for outsourcing entire data centers more traditionally associated with outsourcing. Many organizations are considering outsourcing as a means to handle the increasingly complex technologies supporting data and voice networking.

Choosing services and software to manage these networks poses additional challenges. Some users are letting the provider manage their transmission services, while others are picking and choosing software and services to manage their own networks. As communications remains a vital, costly, and often strategic resource, senior management within organizations no longer assign it a low priority. Rather, they seek to reap the most benefit from their networks at the least cost.

Why Outsource?

With the proliferation of distributed and desktop computing, computer networks have become the primary transport means of moving information both within and outside an organization. According to industry analysts, over the past several years, corporations have spent over 2.5 trillion U.S. dollars in IT related projects and services. Yet white-collar productivity has not kept up with these investments. The current business environment can be summarized as follows.

- continued global expansion of client business
- diversified global providers
- significant negative currency translations
- mature markets cutting cost, inventories, and consumption
- significant competitive and pricing pressures in core business
- stressing ability to discover, develop, or acquire new products
- continued pressure on overhead and administrative costs
- uncertainty over the business environment

Organizations are under constant pressure to cut costs and focus on the company's core competencies. Since network and desktop services are a significant component of the IT expenditure, corporations are looking to outsource these noncore (yet essential!) services, while hoping to benefit from the technological advances without constant capital investments. This chapter will enable the reader to better understand the networking landscape in terms of outsourcing and/or outtasking. It will help IT and network managers better understand the cost structure, service levels, and risks involved.

The IT industry is undergoing significant changes relevant to business environment. Some of the key drivers are

- legacy system transformation
- dramatic IT infrastructure changes
- client/server ramp up and subsequent support structure and costs
- business process and network re-engineering
- data warehouse initiatives
- desktop computing standardization and choice of computing tools and technology
- integrated help desk services
- commodity buying of hardware and infrastructure services

The promise of increased personal productivity has tempted technology consumers to spend more than $440 billion over the past decade in desktop hardware and software, and more than $2.5 trillion on support, administration, and end-user *operations,* according to industry analysts. Because many enterprises do not consider personal computers and networks—inexpensive individually but very expensive in the aggregate—as elements requiring sufficient management, they have substituted serendipity for management practices in their end-user computing deployment, resulting in a huge waste of time and effort that often negates the real benefits of these systems.

The rising interest in network and desktop outsourcing stems primarily from the architectural chaos caused by the IT departments' spending budget shifting out to end-user departments for support of distributed computing. The fundamental driver behind outsourcing *networking management* (networks and desktop) is the *reduction in the total cost of ownership.*

According to industry analysts it is estimated that an average of only 15 to 20 percent is the actual capital expenditure of the total cost of ownership of an IT Infrastructure. The rest consists of support and management costs. Further, it is estimated that 30 to 45 percent is actually spent on managing networks and desktop services.

Outsourcing networked systems management can help users take advantage of the latest technical advances without spending time researching and implementing them. Users can employ a carrier or other service provider not only to manage their telecommunications services and equipment but also to employ the most effective and efficient communications technology available, such as voice processing, toll fraud protection, desktop systems, client/server systems operations and maintenance, and managing multivendor enterprise networks.

Other functions, like call accounting and fault monitoring, can prove tedious and cumbersome and often require a dedicated staff. An outsourcing provider can save the company time and money by compiling the information and issuing routine reports. Small companies cannot always justify the cost of hiring a network manager, but they can afford to hire an outsourcer or service provider to track and report on their networks. Handing complex or time-consuming processes over to a third party can also free up personnel to concentrate on more strategic matters.

Limitations on Outsourcing

Outsourcing is not for every organization, nor is it always implemented efficiently. Fear is the primary reason organizations shy away from outsourcing. Users are afraid of losing control of a vital resource. If their voice or data network failed and was not soon repaired, companies could lose millions of dollars in business; therefore, they do not want to be left with their hands tied when their network fails,. Companies want to know how quickly a service provider will respond to a problem and what that provider can do to promote effective and timely recovery.

Outsourcing networked systems management is not always as cost effective as it may initially appear. Long-term contracts and special requests can run up the costs until they approach what they might have been if the users managed their own networks. Not only that, if a service provider leaves the business, users could find themselves with little recourse, holding responsibility for a crucial resource and technology they no longer understand.

When Do You Outsource?

Like all outsourcing decisions, determining what network and systems management functions to outsource requires intensive investigation.

Some key factors organizations must consider before making an outsourcing decision are highlighted in this section.

The organization must first evaluate its own network, human and equipment resources, company business strategy, future goals, and its ability to meet these future goals with and without outsourcing its network management. Even if the organization chooses not to outsource, the process can prove invaluable since the organization will probably find ways to manage its networks and personnel more effectively.

Effective negotiation can spell success once an organization analyzes its overall operation and sets baselines. Successful negotiation can facilitate an amicable relationship between both parties, which, in turn, promotes better service and response time. It should also define procedures for handling future conflicts as well as upgrading and reconfiguring the network.

Service costs play a key role in the decision-making process. Therefore, organizations should evaluate not only the initial cost versus savings plan but should also carefully evaluate what maintenance will cost over the contract's term, and what additional charges might occur. The outsourcing contract should also impose financial penalties on the provider if performance falls below established minimum standards. The organization should obviously set payment terms and reach a mutually acceptable billing arrangement, guaranteeing that services will be provided on a timely basis with no unknown charges suddenly levied.

Overall successful outsourcing arrangements reach beyond the letter of law to the business relationships and partnerships developed within the member organizations. Realizing that the outsourcing company has to make a profit could quench a customer's unrealistic expectations, while understanding and appreciating the user's business could help the vendor maximize time and effort, making for a satisfied customer.

Networked Systems Management Outsourcing

Networked systems management outsourcing is the process by which an organization contractually and strategically engages an outside service provider who is proficient in the design, development, deployment, operations, and management of networking infrastructure and associated management service applications. The outsourcing relationship includes the following:

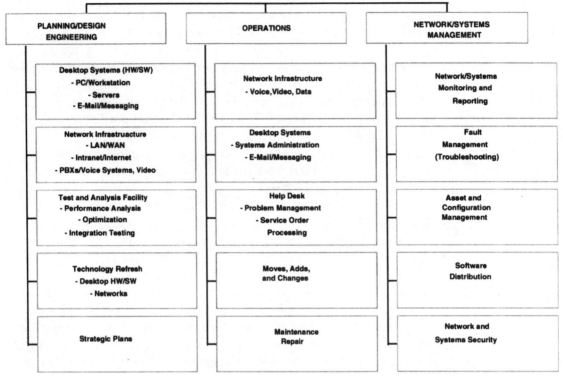

Figure 8.1   Network and Desktop Outsourcing Services

- technical services
- fee for service
- business relationship

Technical Services.   The services provided under the scope of networked system management outsourcing arrangements are illustrated in Figure 8.1

The outsourcing services supplier provides all acquisition, design, operations, and management services related to the following:

Network infrastructure. LANs and WANs, voice, video, data, cable plant, network devices, addressing and transport

Desktop systems. file servers, PCs, workstations, software and peripherals

End-user services. system acquisition, help desk, maintenance and repair

Fee for Service.   The outsourcing arrangement can include any number of pricing mechanisms, including

- fixed price per device or end-user per month
- actual cost of service plus a fee
- actual cost plus share of savings realized between the in-house cost and a predetermined cost reduction program

Most outsourcing engagements include a hybrid pricing approach whereby a fixed price is agreed upon and cost saving initiatives and/or productivity improvements that lead to increased revenue for the outsourced company are shared on a percentage basis.

Business Relationship.   Outsourcing arrangements usually include a business relationship that is structured for the mutual benefit of each party and collectively beneficial to the outsourcing partnership. Examples of business issues to be addressed include the following:

- contractual terms and conditions including contract length, liabilities, and rights of parties
- human resources policies and procedures including compensation, fringe benefits, and severance pay
- service-level agreements including maintenance response time, end-user response and problem resolution time, and service order processing time
- escalation procedures
- subcontractor arrangements
- asset purchase and leaseback options

Types of Networked Systems Management Outsourcing

The term *outsourcing* means different things to different people. Outsourcing's most traditional meaning is used in the IT world where it refers to relinquishing all data processing responsibilities to a third party. The customer thus replaces its internal MIS functions with an external organization, known as a service provider.

The service provider provides all the necessary staffing, often hiring them from the user's own organization. The personnel actually work on site in similar ways to an internal MIS department. This type of outsourcing, also known as facilities management, emerged in the early 1970s as one of the early outsourcing types. Facilities management has increased in recent years to include managing voice and data network infrastructure and further to include managing an organization's entire IT infrastructure.

For some customers, managed network services combine the best of the outsourcing and private networking management worlds. Both communications transport providers and other vendors provide management services for the customer's data and voice networks. Some combine the services and the customer premises equipment required to access them under one umbrella offering, while others offer individual services with varying platforms. The carriers generally provide these services using a backbone network shared by multiple users. Customers own or lease the premises equipment, allowing them to monitor the network, control some functions, and request changes. Some carriers appoint operators to monitor and control the customer's network remotely. Available managed network services range from simple billing reports and configuration management to more sophisticated performance monitoring and problem management.

However, traditionally there are demarcations between the communications infrastructure and its extension into the customers' local area networks and further into the desktop systems. This often creates a rift between the telecommunications service providers and the organization managing the local area networks and desktop systems. There are several new-generation vendors who would manage the entire communications infrastructure, often negotiating service levels with the transport providers and managing their services along with the LANs and the desktop systems. Further, they would also operate and maintain client/server applications and all the associated distributed systems. This provides economies of scale for the customers and a single point of contact and accountability, thus avoiding finger pointing and other associated problems with discrete contracts.

Overall, outsourcing falls into two broad categories. The first can be defined as transferring computer and networking assets, as well as their daily systems operations, management, and personnel, to a third-party provider. In this scenario, outsourcing transfers responsibilities from its internal staff and often the ownership of associated assets—such as computer systems, networking equipment, private branch exchanges—as well.

The other broad category occurs on a smaller scale and on a well-defined vertical scope. Often termed *outtasking*, it involves going out to a service provider for specific management functions; it is the growing trend in the outsourcing industry. Outtasking services are purchased for individual tasks, such as performance reporting, remote backup, help desk

Network Design Services	• Fixed Price • Cost + % of Savings • Cost + fee
Network Management Services	Fixed Price per month (24 x 7 operation) • per managed object/device • per supporting device
Systems Management Services	Fixed price per month (24 x 7 operation) • per managed system • per seat/call • per user
Asset Management Services	Fixed price (24 x 7 operation) • per desktop • per node • per MAC
Internet Services	Fixed Price (24 x 7 operation) • per transaction • per Web page/Hit • per call
Desktop Services	Fixed Priced • per call • per seat, per user, per desktop

Figure 8.2 Network and Desktop Outtasking Services and Pricing Model

or software support, rather than for the entire management and support environment. Outtasking resides somewhere between network integration services and traditional outsourcing, where discrete management services are engaged on a contractual basis.

Companies can select from a variety of outtasking services; often, fees are based on a fixed cost per managed object, making the budgeting process quite manageable. Outtasking companies can offer support levels that most user organizations cannot match, including support for all of the latest popular management software and platforms. Options for support through these providers include quarterly or annual contracts, per-call charges, and/or a fixed price for a specified number of managed objects, support hours, or support incidents. Figure 8.2 illustrates some examples of outtasking services and their pricing models.

Strategic Elements of Outsourcing

Although the carriers are willing to outsource networking management on a large, multinational level, it is not their primary business objective.

Since global communications has emerged as a pending business priority, however, leading interexchange carriers are partnering with international outsourcers to provide multinational outsourcing and networked systems management services. Some strategic elements that customers need to evaluate and think through are outlined in this section. They are by no means complete and the reader is encouraged to refer to other published materials on those subjects.

Network Outsourcing in Network Centric Computing

Corporations are constantly challenged with new technology to aid in the movement and management of information to enable them to attain a competitive edge. However, the cost of infrastructure and network computing resources are escalating due to significant hidden support requirements that are not usually visible during the initial phases of the program.

An increasing number of companies are outsourcing their networking and desktop services to outside firms. Usually, companies that do this have two reasons for doing so: to save on time and to cut on staff and cost. Network outsourcing today is easier, especially with the proliferation of full-service networking service providers who can provide customers with a wide range of services ranging from installation to maintenance.

But when the heart of any corporation's survival is its network (literally dependent on that *network dialtone* for its commerce) would it make sense to depend on an outside vendor to provide that infrastructure? The answer to this question is nontrivial. A close analog to this scenario is when people use telephones to conduct their mission-critical business, but don't own the telecommunications infrastructure (which is provided by a reliable and proven outside carrier). Similarly, several service vendors are deploying network service infrastructure to provide reliable services similar to telephone dialtone.

Economic Drivers for Outsourcing

Cost containment: a commodity approach to the supply and purchase of network and desktop services, where economies of scale offer opportunities for cost reduction that are just not possible internally, even where headcount is optimized by streamlining procedures and then automating as many of the internal operations as possible

Value-based propositions much more creative, both on the account of the outsourcing vendor and the service purchaser where improvements leading to cost savings are shared—with any risk—between parties

The emergence of the internet and intranet as channels for electronic commerce will have implications across the whole demand-supply chain, with the likelihood that desktop applications will increasingly be perceived as front-line business tools, rather than back-office systems. If there is a high level of expectation for network computing, it is not necessarily always matched by a corresponding level of understanding among end-users of network and desktop technology, and it can only become more complex as groupware or internet-enabled applications emerge as realistic options. For the moment, one home truth is that end-users are regularly reported as being continually dissatisfied with the quality of internal IT support, which is criticized as being too reactive.

Service Delivery Using Networks: Where Is the Center of Gravity?

All organizations often struggle to balance their requirements between business management and end-user (customer) management. Each of these segments have differing objectives. Business management is concerned about costs, service delivery, time and shareholder satisfaction while the end-user community is concerned about reliability, frustrations, new technology, and knowledge access. Figure 8.3 describes the bal-

Figure 8.3   Balance Between End-user and Business Management

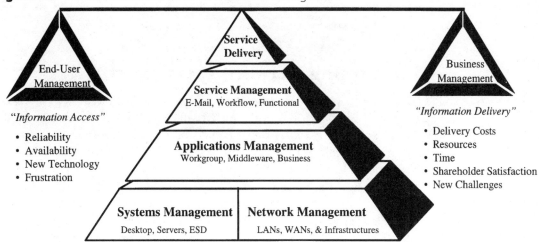

ance that an organization has to develop between its business and end-user objectives, which is oftentimes difficult and confusing. Although most of these requirements are interrelated, they are approached with different thought processes.

Outsourcing aside, there is an unquestioning need for network and desktop technology to be better integrated with business needs to produce innovative solutions in a cost-effective manner. Over the past several years, the capital costs of these technologies have continued to drop. But the complexity of using and supporting these systems has continued to grow, needing more training for end-users and more knowledgeable system administrators. Developments on several fronts will only add to the level of uncertainty over the future of support costs.

Outtasking Network Infrastructure and End-User Computing

Networking has proliferated into several segments of business operations. Most corporations budget a certain amount of support costs for IT, based on certain assumptions. However, the actual support is at least one to two times more than is usually budgeted. This is termed as underground support, which is usually difficult to quantify and document and is a significant drain on corporate capital and resources.

Organizations need to address issues related to the support of network and desktop services and how to capture costs associated with certain tasks. Some vendors are ahead in this new-wave service strategy known as outtasking. This usually involves well-defined deliverables for specific tasks associated with end-to-end information movement and management process and/or IT service delivery.

Outsourcing Network Infrastructure

Organizations need to evaluate and explore different technologies related to network and desktop services. Service delivery models need to be established. Partnership approaches need to be described where the vendors work with the clients to streamline and standardize network and desktop infrastructure.

Analysts and market researchers have long been predicting an upturn in the demand for network and desktop outsourcing services on the basis that contracting out can offer immediate improvements in the quality of voice, data and video services and the longer-term promise of better value for money. Some 35 percent of organizations outsource the design, implementation, and/or operation of their corporate networks.

In truth, there are all sorts of triggers to network outsourcing, and most of them are being set off by one strong overriding concern: maintaining the technical skills to manage the complexity of the corporate network is becoming more demanding by the day. And then there are the considerations of emerging technologies like frame relay, ATM, desktop video conferencing, and mobile computing.

While it may be the case that these new services offer opportunities for improved services, greater functionality, better performance, and lower running costs, it is also true that—to greater or lesser degrees—they involve some level of capital investment. Businesses are reviewing their capital investment with a microscope.

Moves to client/server, access-to-remote and distributed-data networks, internet computing, and multimedia-capable desktops all have big implications for networking that are difficult to interpret or predict. All this suggest that the entire networking infrastructure could easily be outsourced to an outside vendor with sufficient management controls.

Cost Models and Third-Wave Pricing

Organizations and outsourcing vendors, together, need to define the cost driver of the current setup of corporate network and desktop infrastructure. Organizations need to understand how services should be tariffed and how pricing needs to be structured in the outsourcing deal. How change will be managed and priced must be thought through. And many other considerations like penalty clauses, services threshold limits, and exit costs need to be described.

Before outsourcing alternatives can be properly considered, it is necessary first to fully articulate the cost of network services and desktop computing, taking in the cost of procurement, installation, support, maintenance, software updates, network audit, and asset management. In addition, some form of financial model will be needed before decisions can be made about outsourcing.

Cost models are required to describe the outsourcing process that includes many factors that are often overlooked: the cost of travel to remote sites, the cost of unsupported upgrades, the average fault call time, the number of nonnetworked desktops, the cost of audit—every factor needs to be taken into account. Figures 8.4 and 8.5 describe some representative samples of pricing and costing models.

SIZE/OPERATION (managed objects) / SERVICE	24 X 7 OPERATION			12 X 5 OPERATION		
	0 - 300	301 - 600	> 600	0 - 300	301 - 600	> 600
NETWORK MANAGEMENT						
SYSTEMS MANAGEMENT						
ASSET MANAGEMENT						

Figure 8.4   Pricing and Operating Model for Outsourcing Services

Risks and Rewards of Network and Desktop Outsourcing

Unlike other outsourcing fields, like the facilities management of the IT data center, there are very few suppliers that could take on the management of an entire network single-handedly. This is an area that calls for *smart sourcing*, where specific aspects of networking management and

Figure 8.5

Examples of Pricing Models for Internet, Help Desk, and Full Life Cycle Desktop Services

VOLUME/ SIZE (users) / SERVICE	24 X 7 OPERATION			
	0 - 500	501 - 1000	1001 - 5000	> 5 k
Internet				
Help Desk				
Desktop Services				

desktop services (notably all the time-consuming tasks, help desk, technology refresh, maintenance, and some specialized and highly complex tasks) are outsourced to service suppliers.

Organizations need to understand the various risks and rewards associated with outsourcing the network and desktop infrastructure, in terms of

- opportunities versus threats
- reduced costs versus cost escalation
- improved value for money versus dilution of technical capability
- increased flexibility versus significant "change" costs
- access to new technology versus loss of staff morale and specialist skills
- transition difficulties versus fee for service

Who Is in Charge?

Structuring a networking and desktop services outsourcing deal is a non-trivial task. Flexibility to renegotiate after a couple of years would be ideal as both technology and business climates tend to change every 18 to 24 months. Termination for cause, convenience, and change of control should be essential terms of an outsourcing deal. Organizations need to understand the various "soft" issues that need to be taken into consideration. In addition, organizations need to evaluate and explore the various options in structuring a deal so that they will have sufficient control over the engagement. Service level models need to be described. Quality assurance and audit rights need to be thought through.

The Outsourcing Process

As illustrated in Figure 8.6, the implementation of an outsourcing relationship requires a number of preliminary activities that ultimately lead to an outsourcing contract. Depending on the scope of the outsourcing initiative (e.g., network, desktop, networking management, applications, and/or data center), the outsourcing process itself may last from three to eight months. A representative outsourcing schedule is illustrated in Figure 8.7.

Critical to the long-term success of the outsourcing engagement is the due diligence phase and subsequent transition process. During the due

Figure 8.6
The Outsourcing
Process

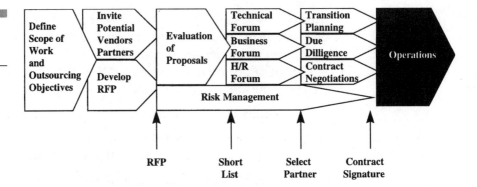

diligence process, the outsourcing vendor must gather all of the information required to support its proposed technical service model and pricing structure. This information resides in a variety of locations in various formats and includes, for example, number and type of personal computers by location, software used, network devices, current configurations, service levels in place, current subcontractors, asset value and depreciation schedules, and so forth. During the contract transition phase, critical success factors include a well-defined baseline, detailed project planning, and open lines of communications.

Networked systems management outsourcing consists of the following functions related to the IT infrastructure and the required services that an outsourcer needs to provide at a minimum as part of the overall network management and operations. These functions should include on-site and remote delivery of LAN/WAN-related services that deliver superior functionality in availability, usability, performance, security, adaptability, and price.

Figure 8.7
Sample Timetable
for an Outsourcing
Engagement

• **Develop RFP**	1 to 2 Months
• **Vendor Response Development**	1 Month
• **Proposal Review and Evaluation**	1 Month
• **Due Diligence**	1 to 2 Months
• **SelectFinalist**	2 Weeks
• **Contract Negotiation/Transition Planning**	1 Month

Configuration Management. CM is responsible for detecting, controlling, and administering the state of the network.

- single point of contact
- capture and maintenance of configuration database
- configuration of data reports
- coordination of moves/adds/changes
- equipment provisioning
- testing moves/adds/changes
- status reporting on network changes
- problem tracking, escalation, and resolution
- software distribution
- software licensing
- server administration: network operating system, backup and recovery
- desktop software administration

Performance Management. PM analyzes and controls throughput and error rates on the network. It captures, maintains, and updates historical information to plot trends and provide management recommendations.

- identify performance needs
- define data to be captured
- capture and maintain database of performance metrics and measurements
- package performance data for modeling tools
- provide periodic reporting and analysis to improve network performance
- submit customer-accessible performance data and reports
- identify unique monitoring needs
- establish thresholds and alarm rates for network performance
- provide performance analysis for all managed devices
  - network traffic analysis
  - trend analysis
  - protocol analysis
  - throughput analysis
  - utilization analysis

Fault Management.   FM is responsible for detecting, isolating, controlling, and resolving errant network behavior in both a proactive and reactive manner and then reporting incidents to the customer. Trouble ticketing is a subset service.

- single point of contact
- fault isolation and diagnosis
- initiation of corrective actions through a third party or directly
- fault reporting to the customer of all errant network behavior
- creation and maintenance of trouble-ticket database
- periodic FM report generation (problem and trouble-ticket reports, vendor performance reports)
- customized reports
- preemptive/predictive fault analysis
- identification of unique monitoring needs
- vendor management (dispatch, problem escalation, and maintenance of vendor database)
- problem tracking, escalation and resolution
- establishment of thresholds and alarm rates
- direct customer access to fault and trouble-ticket information
- coordination of faults with networking management partners

Security Management.   SM provides ongoing protection of the network and its components by analyzing and minimizing risks, implementing the network security plan, and monitoring the implementation of the plan.

- monitoring of network log-on, password, security indicator surveillance
- partitioning
- development and deployment of violation indicators
- security management report generation
- proactive security measures (termination of access, recording illegal access, determining the access point, and apprehending the violator)
- implementation and maintenance of encryption techniques
- creation and maintenance of network security log
- on-going security analysis to minimize risk
- development and implementation of ongoing security plans

An outsourcing vendor's typical approach is described in the following section as a reference for both providers and user organizations.

Outsourcing Approach: A Business Partnership

An outsourcing vendor's approach to network and systems management should be based on developing a strategic relationship with their clients—a true business partnership whereby risks and rewards are jointly shared. For a vendor, a successful business partnership based on providing high-quality networked systems management outsourcing services should include the following:

- open lines of communication at all times
- an understanding of the customer's business objectives in order to align IT services accordingly
- ensuring a flexible, responsive human resources model during transition and ongoing operations
- continuously focusing on relationships throughout all layers of the client's organization
- being flexible, creative, and responsive in providing technical solutions including gain-sharing initiatives

Managing distributed networked systems will continue to be a challenge as the underlying technologies become increasingly complex. Based on this trend, and the need for organizations to focus on their core business competencies in an increasingly competitive marketplace, the networked systems management outsourcing industry will continue to grow as well. In addition, internet service options and the increase in corporate intranets will require even experienced service providers to continuously expand their outsourcing capabilities and services.

SUMMARY

A major transformation is taking place in the way companies are deciding what, when, and with whom to outsource. How these services are procured and managed is changing, too. Major changes are also occurring in the marketplace as new entrants emerge and vendors form situational alliances for the lifetime of a single deal. Companies must carefully evaluate the ability of their prospective vendors to provide services effectively as well as efficiently over the life of the deal.

In summary, the reasons for outsourcing are changing, the nature of outsourcing is changing, and the ways vendors relate to network and desktop outsourcing clients continue to change. Outsourcing network and desktop infrastructure is a *strategic* concept—a way to add value to the business that converts an in-house cost center into a customer-focused service operation.

CHAPTER 9

Conclusions

Introduction

On balance, given the business realities, one finds that information-based electronic linkages are fast becoming the glue that binds companies together and fosters partnerships. Such links that facilitate the generation, use, and storage of information and knowledge have been gaining importance for some time now. Disparate business entities can now act in concert as a single competitor by leveraging electronic value-added links. There are significant advantages in using electronic networks as the linchpin for exchanging information, engaging the market, and providing services. This chapter will discuss characteristics of global information networks and services that are delivered using those networks. In addition, we will discuss the business impacts of the networks and how such enabling technologies as asynchronous transfer mode (ATM), frame relay, network applications and internet (and intranet) will constantly challenge IT managers to keep up with these dynamics.

Networked Systems— A Business Imperative

The demands on and for global networking capability are intensifying. This evolution, both within and outside the United States, reflects the changing character of business across the globe. Multinational corporations are reorganizing to take advantage of global opportunities. Corporate finance, logistics, telecommunications, call centers, and IS functions are being centralized on a worldwide or a continental basis, while activities involving direct customer interaction are more regionalized or localized. Global companies are literally following the sun to take advantage of local time zones and competitive resources that are required to deliver their services.

Companies are working more directly with suppliers and customers. Electronic commerce—e.g., providing on-line access to orders, plans, and forecasts—is now a critical element in both single-country and global business strategies. Imports and exports represent a growing portion of national incomes. These changes have not gone unnoticed by service providers, applications developers, telecommunication carriers, or national governments. Competition is spreading throughout the world, but the pace is far from uniform. Significant infrastructure investments are being made to develop global networks so that companies can use them to run their mission-critical applications and enable employees to move information across and among their customers, trading partners, and suppliers. These networks have become not only a survival tool but even more so a competitive weapon.

These dynamics highlight the importance of having a flexible global network strategy. In many respects, the efforts mirror what occurs in domestic network planning, but there are critically important differences. A network strategy has two major components. The first is a set of guidelines or principles that are not necessarily technical in nature; usually, they constitute service definitions and the components required to deliver those services. The second component is technical. It begins with a whole-system architecture, a framework of how all the network's piece-parts fit together. Standards are identified, and a detailed description of all services and business applications with supporting protocols and technologies is architected. As Figure 9.1 describes, in any enterprise information network, there are four distinct components that make up the service delivery vehicle: networks (LANs, WANs, etc.), systems (desktops, mainframes, minis, etc.), applications (standard,

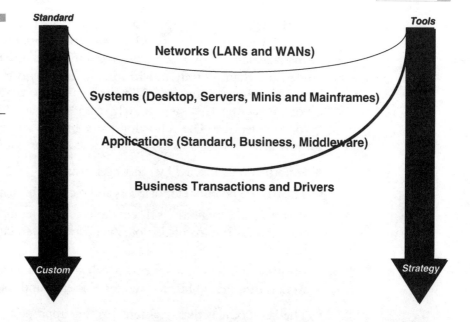

Figure 9.1
Components and Customization Required for Networking Service Delivery

Standard · Tools

Networks (LANs and WANs)

Systems (Desktop, Servers, Minis and Mainframes)

Applications (Standard, Business, Middleware)

Business Transactions and Drivers

Custom · Strategy

middleware, business), and business transactions and drivers. As one moves from infrastructure components (like networks and systems) to business processes and transactions, it is imperative that the management and operation of the enterprise networks be customized to the specific organization. The way these components are integrated is also usually tailored to an organization.

Managing Global Networks— No Serendipity

Corporate IT managers are familiar with the problems associated with extending a local network-based system into the wide area—typically performance, cost, and availability. These same issues apply when national networks are extended globally. One of the most important trends seen over recent years has been the increasing lack of distinction between LANs and internetworks and WANs, a pattern that has recently been extended to global networks as well. In addition it is a challenging time of transition as enterprises globalize their business operations without putting sufficient thought into the expansion capabilities of their information network infrastructures.

With the increasing importance of enterprise management, many vendors of LAN and WAN network management systems have been adding in management of more device types and wider internetworking capabilities, and then proudly proclaiming their systems to be "integrated" or "enterprise." In addition, even IT managers believe that when they have a lot of interconnected boxes, they have an "integrated" networking strategy or architecture. The following are some key issues that need to be addressed when networks are expanded to support global operations.

- Performance is affected by the longer distances.
- There is the potential for data loss and security breaches.
- Protocols and applications that are interactive—requiring extensive back-and-forth transmission of small packets—can be expensive to maintain.
- Imaging and workflow systems, which generate a great deal of network traffic, should be reviewed for efficiency and robustness.

The key point is that decisions that are appropriate for domestic networks are not necessarily transferable to global networks. It is also critical for network planners and designers to know the directions being contemplated by the business strategy and operating departments—for example, if expansion in specific parts of the world, or outsourcing certain functions of the enterprise, is under consideration. These issues are very important to consider in expanding the underlying information network infrastructure.

SUMMARY

The combination of using a common management information repository, an expert system, and a management platform provides a greater degree of multivendor integration than any one scheme. In the manager-of-managers architecture, interactions among management systems from different vendors are accomplished through a standardized protocol interface and a standardized set of management data definitions. This hierarchical way of aggregating management information requires that a single vendor—the provider of the integrator—develop all the multivendor management application software. Other vendors merely provide raw data to the integrated manager, and accept commands, both through open interfaces.

Independently, whether the manager-of-managers or the platform approach, or a combination of the two is selected, the ultimate goal should be to manage a multivendor, multi-service network. Vendors may support proprietary, de facto, or open standards at the managed objects or management application level. Cross-connection via proxy engines is required to support certain managed objects or when implementing management systems for an existing network consisting of proprietary components.

Many paradigms have been proposed, but only a few have caught on when it comes to technology upgrade and deployment. When contrasted to the progress of hardware technology or software technology by itself, networking management technology evolution is puzzling. The reason lies in the essential difference between pure software and hardware and a combination of software, hardware, and networking management application technology—a difference that requires a paradigm shift and a robust architectural strategy for networking management takes much longer. In order to implement networking management technology for distributed systems networks, one must not only develop new architectures and framework but also bring about changes in the job function of network operators.

It is also extremely important to involve the end-user of these systems upfront during the technology selection and system design phase. In addition, continuous involvement of the end-users (network operators) is crucial for successful deployment of new technology and architectures. At the technology deployment and transfer stage, emphasis should be on end-user benefits, not on the new technology. Usually, new technology is perceived as loss of jobs. This perception should be addressed as early as possible. Oftentimes it is difficult to grasp the end-user's perception of the problem and to transfer the technology without help. This could be solved by having a coordinator who is intimately familiar and is part of the user's work habits and culture. Knowing the management system user's perception of the problem early in the development stage can help ensure a successful technology and network management application deployment. This is especially true when some of this new network management technology is object oriented and is used to solve some of the biggest challenges of managing distributed networked systems.

We have proven that we can develop complex networking management applications using technological tools. Now we have to rearrange the way we work to use them effectively. New technological tools empower network managers and operators by expanding the availability of information related to the network. Some crucial decision making related to the network are simplified because of the raise in the comfort level due to the availability of critical information.

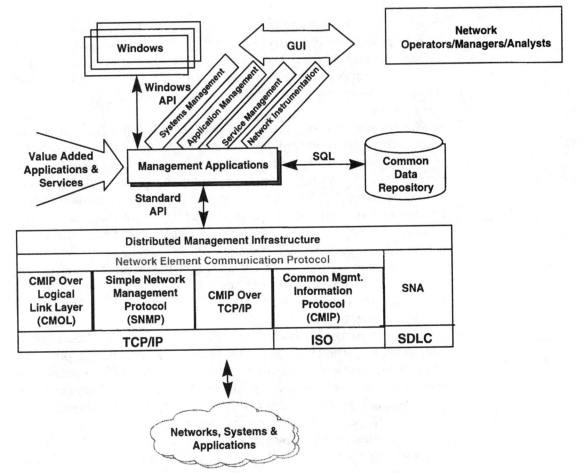

Figure 9.2 Integrated Management Framework

Sophisticated technologies are also changing relationships among people in distributed organizations. Supervisors once understood the work that was done by their teams. That may not be the case now. For example, workers often understand the techniques used in advanced networking management systems better than managers. This trend gives employees more control and empowers them to expand their roles and responsibilities. An overall framework and architecture for integrated management of distributed networked systems are depicted in Figure 9.2 and Figure 9.3 respectively.

New technologies will have a tremendous impact on organizations. New tools should not be used to do what has always been done. Instead they should be used to help redesign the way the networked system is

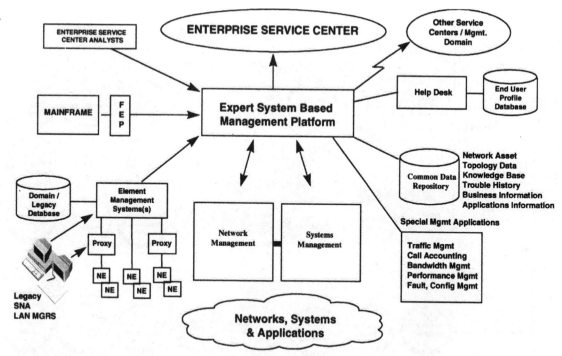

Figure 9.3 *Overall Architecture for Integrated Networked Systems Management*

managed and controlled. But caution should be exercised when deploying new technology. It is crucial that the end-user is involved upfront in the decision process and also trained well. Further, there should be frequent interaction with the end-user to discuss the implications of new technologies and how they can help achieve the overall networking management objectives and goals.

No single development methodology can address all the issues associated with large-scale networking management system development. But having an architectural strategy (and being flexible), prototyping, and frequent end-user interaction were found to be the best ways to deploy a *functional* management system quickly, in addition to significantly reducing the system development time. Developing wrong functions, unacceptable user interfaces, trying to solve all the problems at once, dealing with *needs* rather than *wants*, and coping with a stream of requirements changes can all work to destabilize the technology and system deployment. A representative sample of a development methodology is illustrated in Figure 9.4 which depicts some parallel activities in the design, development, and testing phases of the management system infrastructure.

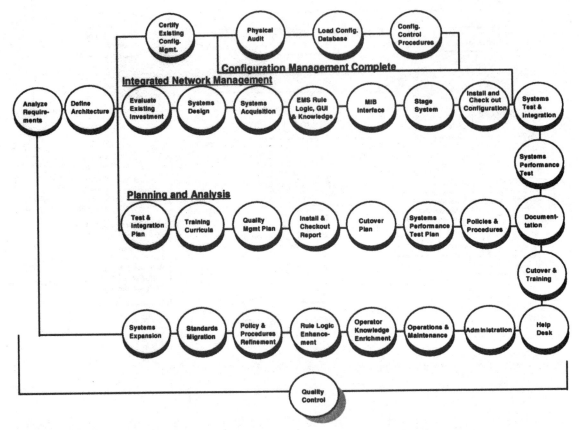

Figure 9.4   A Sample Development Methodology

Managing globally distributed networks is nontrivial and frequently challenging. The design of an integrated management system is the transformation of a problem (often inconsistent and chaotic) from the real network control center to the service world. Networking management systems must evolve as management applications and end-user needs are better understood, with provision made for validation and evolution. The focus for managing distributed networks should be to leverage low-cost powerful computers and a toolkit to create and deliver enterprise-specific management service applications, pioneer and control networking management paradigms, and develop systems engineering and integration expertise that creates enduring influence and value to end-users. This focus does not undermine the efforts involved in actual system development, but hides it somewhat due to the use of object-oriented methodology. Instead, the emphasis shifts to architectural and design matters.

The system needed to manage a globally distributed network need not be built from scratch. Instead, it could be a combination of systems engineering, integration, and necessary development to address specific and unique characteristics and peculiarities of the network. With the systemic approach described in this book, managing distributed networked systems would consist of several phases. This is because implementing a real-time expert system for intelligent management needs to keep pace with significant network events. The management system must be flexible and robust enough for handling an avalanche of network events such as those caused by node failure without simply giving up and failing at such a crucial moment. It is necessary to build or provide an intermediate alarms filter to handle some frequent events (distributed management). Thus a local *intelligent agent* can perform very useful temporal reasoning, and try to solve the problem before passing the new or escalated event to a higher *global expert system* with greater (more information) reasoning capabilities.

Many of the concepts and design examples described in this book are generic to any distributed network, and represent an evolutionary approach for building sophisticated management applications for different networking environments. Examples of some concepts and design approaches are the segmentation of network errors into proactively and reactively generated, novel design and use of the network application and fault manager, the multiparadigm knowledge representation approach, the design and implementation of a CMIR, and above all the concept of hierarchical escalation of events and alarms. In addition, defining a robust and flexible architecture allows one to build additional management service applications without worrying about user interface, communication protocols, database interfaces, and interfaces between different management service applications. The potential impact of an intelligent and integrated management system in a distributed networked system domain is enormous and provides significant opportunities for managing complex network management issues.

Managing a sophisticated distributed network is nontrivial when it involves standard (such as SNMP) and nonstandard devices and equipment. In addition each type of device or network component has its own element management system, and the challenge is to integrate them while distributing the management functionality.

The emphasis in the overall development effort and project cycle is on increasing value to the end-user rather than merely expanding the designer's intellectual horizons and interests. The value that is mentioned here is in the development of various management service applications using off-the-shelf tools, APIs, and rapid development methodology. The integrated management system is implemented using a client/server model while distributing the management functionality. In the coming years, organizations with good integration skills will have a tremendous advantage, and vendors having the tools to implement the client/server solutions and API will serve their customers best.

The rapidly changing networking environments and the emergence of sophisticated distributed applications place an ever-increasing burden on currently available networking management products. No single vendor can provide a complete solution to manage such networks. Flexibility to change is difficult to manage as the quantity and types of managed objects explode. The principal effect of incorporating higher flexibility into networking management systems is the increased complexity of those systems and poses a greater challenge to designers and integrators to keep it under control. To further complicate matters, there is a growing demand for customized management systems using standard tools to conform to the requirements of individual organizations.

As we better understand management problems associated with distributed networks, the focus shifts towards the operations and control aspects of networking management in real time. There is an increasing need for dynamic collaboration between management systems and between manager and agent systems requiring intelligent and sophisticated filtering and efficient decision making in a short time. Increased complexity requires distributing the management functionality to cooperating and autonomous intelligent agents.

The intelligent and integrated management system described and discussed in this book is general to many distributed and client/server networked systems. The concepts and design considerations are subject to many other constraints, such as user sophistication, test data availability, network management interfaces to both intelligent and nonintelligent devices, and reliability and timeliness of alarms and configuration data. Any of these might prove more daunting than the design of the management system itself. The key to success may lie in selecting sufficiently flexible building blocks with which to build the integrated management infrastructure. When it comes to problem isolation in a heterogeneous set of client/server components that comprise a network, exceptions are the rule. Therefore a combination of approaches may be required. Experience dictates that a general object-oriented approach, in conjunction with a platform technology, offers the greatest latitude in designing real-time expert system-based integrated management system.

Careful thought should be given to knowledge representation and the reasoning paradigm of the expert system architecture versus the overall networking management paradigm established. This is because most of the expert system software that is commercially available evolved from other applications such as control systems, chemical process plants, etc. An object-oriented design allows the convenient representation of the behavior of various service components in the network. An integration with graphical language or a fourth-generation language allows the domain and the model to be defined using create, clone, and connect methodology. With this approach, values can be passed via object connections, thereby providing a graphical means to develop a diagnostic methodology and knowledge representation. With real-time management applications, the reasoning must frequently consider the behavior over time, and usually requires consideration of dynamic models of expected behavior of network service applications.

Finally, real-time problem isolation requires consideration of many issues, such as unsolicited events, the temporary nature of *truth*, the need to achieve a best resolution technique or method in a certain time allocated, the ability to reason efficiently with thousands of objects and rules, and other technical aspects due to the specific architecture of globally distributed networks.

Final Word

There are definite limits on the capability of the existing management platforms, protocol converters, expert system technology, database integration, and other off-the-shelf management applications. Several popular misconceptions must also be considered. The intelligent and integrated networking management system in this book describes management applications where a commercially available expert system software platform was used in implementation—that is, an expert system with a lot of valid knowledge that helped to boost performance beyond what a human operator could achieve alone. These applications require substantial effort by architects, systems engineers, developers, and knowledge engineers to define and validate the system and the KB.

A misconception sometimes exists that the expert system may solve difficult network problems that the operators or engineers do not know how to solve. This is currently beyond the state of the art because expert systems are not yet knowledgeable about target applications. They only provide a means for automation or quick data analysis and decision making. A network model of what is to be learned, with some set of parameters and structures prespecified needs to be defined. An objective function that measures the closeness of fit between the internal model and the measured behavior is nontrivial. A current example of the learning methodology is neural networks, which have achieved some good success integrated with expert systems. This could be extended to solve complex management problems associated with exploding multimedia and internet networks.

The most serious limitation of expert systems is that, although they may do well when confronted with the anticipated network problems, they may fail to understand unanticipated problems. The human expert's power to reason by analogy, to solve unanticipated problems, is superior and should never be compromised. Thus the expert system may be faster to diagnose, and more constantly attentive compared to the human, but the expert system cannot match the reasoning capability of a human expert.

Finally, because mission-critical networks such as networking services require mission-critical networked system management applications, they must be highly available. Object database management system (ODBMS), a fourth-generation DBMS that combines direct modeling of complex, graph-structured data with the power of today's leading object programming languages, offers a powerful combination of management platform, database technology, and real-time expert system shells to develop an even more robust networking management system. Though there are many different types of networking management applications, a common set of core networking management requirements can easily be identified for a given type of networked system. For example, networking management systems tend to model complex data, demand high performance, and require sophisticated software building blocks.

BIBLIOGRAPHY

Ananthanpillai, Raj, *Intelligent and Integrated Management of an Electronic Messaging Services Network*, IEEE Network Operations and Management Symposium, April 1992.

Ananthanpillai, Raj, *Intelligent and Integrated Management of Messaging Networks—Tutorial*, International Symposium Integrated Network Management, San Francisco, April 1993.

Ananthanpillai, Raj, *Managing Messaging Networks—A Systemic Approach*, Artech House, 1995.

Bailey, Angela, "Integrated Network Management," Datapro Information Services Group, The McGraw-Hill Companies, November 1994.

Black, Uyless, *Network Management Standards*, McGraw-Hill, 1992.

Black, Uyless, *TCP/IP and Related Protocols*, McGraw-Hill, 1992.

Carter, Elston, and Januario P. Dia, *Integrated Network Management*, Elsevier Science Publishers, 1991.

Case, J.D., M. Fedor, M.L. Schoffstall, and C. Davin, "Simple Network Management Protocol (SNMP)," RFC 1157, May 1990.

Castle, *E-Mail*, Artech House, 1987.

Datapro, "Artificial Intelligence and Network Management," NM20-200, McGraw-Hill Inc., 1992.

Datapro, "Integrated Network Management," NM40-300, McGraw-Hill, 1992.

Datapro, "Management by Preparedness," NM10-100, McGraw-Hill, 1991.

Datapro, "Network Management Functions," NM20-100, McGraw-Hill, 1991.

Davin, J.J. Galvin, and K. Mcloghrie, "SNMP Administrative Model," RFC 1351, July 1992.

Davis. D, "Artificial Intelligence Goes to Work," *High Technology*, April 1987.

Debenham, John, *Knowledge Systems Design*, Prentice-Hall, 1989.

DeJager, S. Dale, "Experiences in Interface Design," *Unix Review*, March 1987.

Ericson, Ericson, and Minoli, *Expert Systems Applications in Integrated Network Management*, Artech House, 1989.

Faulkner Research Report, Abbott, Lawrence, ed. "Real Products Managing Real Networks," *Managing Distributed Systems*, Vol. IV, No. 8, August 1996.

Gensym Corporation, "G2 Reference Manual," Cambridge, Mass.

Halsall and Modiri, "An Implementation of an OSI Network Management System," *IEEE Network Magazine*, July 1990.

Hecht, B., and C. Miller, Network Systems Management Operations, Gartner Group, September 1994.

Herman, James, and Curtis, Christine, "The Challenge of Managing Broadband Networks," *Business Communications Review*, October 1995.

Huntington-Lee, Jill, "Network Management Functions," Datapro Information Services Group, The McGraw-Hill Companies, March 1996.

IEEE 1992 Network Operations and Management Symposium, Proceedings of the symposium, Vol. 1, 2, and 3.

IEEE Communication Magazine, "OSI Network Management Systems," Vol. 31, May 1993.

IEEE Network Magazine, "The Future of The Internet Protocol," Vol. 7, May 1993.

"Internet Network Management Systems," Datapro Information Services Group, The McGraw-Hill Companies, July 1995.

Jackson, Lynne Marie, "Outsourcing Network Management," Datapro Information Services Group, The McGraw-Hill Companies, February 1995.

Jordaan, J.F., and M.E. Paterok, "Event Correlation in Heterogeneous Networks Using the OSI Management Framework," *Integrated Network Management III*, 1993.

Joseph, C.A., and K.H. Muralidhar, "Integrated Network Management in an Enterprise Environment," *IEEE Network Magazine*, July 1990.

Krishnan, I., and W. Zimmer, *Integrated Network Management II*, Elsevier Science Publishers, 1991.

Krishnan, I., and W. Zimmer, *Integrated Network Management III*, Elsevier Science Publishers, 1993.

Linticum, David S., "Managing Networks," Datapro Information Services Group, The McGraw-Hill Companies, September 1995.

Marques. T.E., "A Real-Time Interactive Expert System for Isolating Faults in Data Networks," IEEE NOMS 88 Conference Record, February 1988.

Marques. T.E., "A Symptom-Driven Expert System for Isolating and Correcting Network Faults," *IEEE Communications Magazine,* March 1988.

Meyer, M.H., K.F. Curley, "Putting Expert Systems Technology to Work," *Sloan Management Review,* Winter 1991.

Miller, M.A., *Managing Internetworks with SNMP,* M&T Books, New York, 1993.

Moore, R.L., "Expert Systems in Real-Time Applications: Experiences and Opportunities," Proceedings of the 17th Annual Advanced Control Conference, Indiana, 1991.

Moore, R.L., and H.P. Rosenof, *Implementing on-line Real-Time Expert Systems,* Gensym Corporation, Cambridge, Mass.

Mouftah, H.T., "Expert Systems for the Performance Evaluation of Communication Networks," IEEE ICC'88 Conference Record, 1988.

"Network Management: Key Issues," Datapro Computer Systems Analyst, The McGraw-Hill Companies, September 1995.

Network Systems Management Operations, Gartner Group, September 1994.

Network World Magazine, "I-NET Unveils Data Repository, Applications Management Service," September 11, 1995.

Network World Magazine, "New Directions in Network Management," Supplement, 1993.

Network World Magazine, Vol. 10, Nos. 7 and 24, February 1993 and August 1993.

Noren, C.S., "Rapid Prototyping Network Management Systems," IEEE Milcom '88.

Olson, L, and A. Blackwell, "Understanding Network Management with OOA," *IEEE Network Magazine,* July 1990.

Open Software Foundation, "The OSF Distributed Management Environment: A White Paper," Cambridge, Mass., January 1991.

Owen, Jeffrey, "Real-World Network Management," Datapro Information Services Group, The McGraw-Hill Companies, August 1995.

Pagurek, B, and A.R. Kaye, "Knowledge Based Fault Location in a Data Communication Network," IEEE ICC'88 Conference Record, 1988.

Rose, M., *The Simple Book,* Prentice Hall, 1991.

Rose, M.T., ed., "Convention for Defining Traps for Use with the SNMP," RFC 1215, March 1991.

Schicker, P., and E. Stefferund, eds., *Message Handling Systems: An Application Layer Protocol*, Elsevier Science Publishers, 1991.

Sevcik, Peter, "The Importance of a Network Architecture," *Business Communications Review*, October 1995.

Stallings, W., *SNMP, SNMPv2, and CMIP—The Practical Guide to Network Management Standards*, Addison-Wesley, Reading, Mass., 1993.

Terdiman, R., and A. Cushman, "Outsourcing Vendor Evaluation and Selection Process," Gartner Group, March 1996.

Tienari, Martii, and Dipak Khakar, eds., *Information Networks and Data Communication IV*, Elsevier Science Publishers, 1992.

Upp, Michael, "Physical Network Management: An Essential Tool for Managing Growing Networks," *International Journal of Network Management*, Vol. 3, March 1993.

Vesonder, G.T., "Rule-based Programming in the UNIX System," *AT&T Technical Journal* 67(1), February, 1988, pp. 69—80.

Wescott, Jill, et al., "Automated Network Management," IEEE Proceedings INFOCOM, 1985.

INDEX

About the Author

Raj Ananthanpillai is the founder, president, and CEO of NETSOLV Corporation, an enterprise asset management company. Before starting this company, he was the senior vice president of corporate strategy and marketing at I-NET, Inc. where he was responsible for developing new products, services, markets, strategic business alliances, and overall strategy. Prior to this, he was the vice president and general manager of I-NET's enterprise networking management services business unit. Before joining I-NET, he spent several years at AT&T where his last responsibility was directing and managing global messaging network management activities at their EasyLink services business unit. He holds an M.Sc. in Engineering Physics (Kakatiya University, India), an MS in Electrical Engineering (University of Kansas), and a mini-MBA in Global Business from George Washington University and AT&T school of business. Raj has a patent on distributed applications management related work and has authored another book in the area of information systems management. He is widely quoted in industry publications.